Social Welfare and the Future of the State

Social Welfare and the Failure of the State

*Centralised Social Services and
Participatory Alternatives*

ROGER HADLEY
STEPHEN HATCH

London
GEORGE ALLEN & UNWIN
Boston   Sydney

First published in 1981

GEORGE ALLEN & UNWIN LTD
40 Museum Street, London WC1A 1LU

© Roger Hadley and Stephen Hatch, 1981

British Library Cataloguing in Publication Data
Hadley, Roger
    Social welfare and the failure of the state.
    1. Public welfare – Great Britain – History
    I. Title   II. Hatch, Stephen
    361'.941   HV245

    ISBN 0–04–361049–8
    ISBN 0–04–361050–1 Pbk

Set in 11 on 12 point Times by Computacomp (UK) Ltd,
Fort William, Scotland
and printed in Great Britain
by Biddles Ltd, Guildford, Surrey

Contents

Preface

Our decision to write this book was made in 1978. We had recently contributed to the Wolfenden Report, *The Future of Voluntary Organisations*, Roger Hadley as a member of the Wolfenden Committee and Stephen Hatch as its research officer, and we felt it was important to develop some of the ideas raised by the committee. In particular it was our view that the committee had not taken far enough its critique of the way social policy had evolved since the war, nor had it blazoned an alternative vision of the future.

Our belief in the need for a reappraisal of the role of the state in social welfare has been reinforced by changes that have taken place since 1978. These have brought the country to an intellectual bankruptcy such that the main argument about policies for the 1980s is between protagonists of the policies of the 1920s and protagonists of the policies of the 1940s. This book has been written in the hope that it will help to steer political debate on to new ground.

The Joseph Rowntree Memorial Trust has played a crucial if unwitting role in the conception of the book, first by establishing the Committee on the Future of Voluntary Organisations and subsequently by making possible the formation of the Voluntary Organisations Research Unit. We are grateful to the trust, and also to Morag McGrath, Roger Sherrott and Paul Wilding for their comments on the drafts: none of them, however, bears any responsibility for the final product. In the typing of the manuscript we have been helped by a number of people, among whom we owe a special debt to Ruby Bendall and Wendy Hopfl.

ROGER HADLEY
STEPHEN HATCH

CHAPTER 1

Introduction

During the past two decades discussion of social policy in Britain has been dominated by the assumption that the state should occupy the central place in the provision of social services. The character of this discussion has owed much to the influence of one man, Richard Titmuss, and his followers. Titmuss, who was professor of social administration at the London School of Economics from 1951 to 1973, had a profound mistrust of the market and placed powerful emphasis in his writing on the use of the state to redistribute resources in favour of equality. The state, he argued, should play a strongly integrative role, in particular compensating for the adverse effects of social and economic change. While not suggesting that the policies advocated by Titmuss have found universal acceptance, few of the large number of professionals who have entered the social services in recent years can have been immune to the intellectual climate he did so much to create.

Between 1961 and 1976 the proportion of the growing gross national product absorbed by public expenditure on the social services rose from 17 per cent to 28 per cent. Titmuss's doctrines served to legitimate this extension of the activities of the state. But this has not meant that the goals implied by these doctrines have actually been achieved. Certainly the extent of inequality has remained obstinately immune to more than marginal alteration. Arguments about the integrative function of statutory services were given a new dimension as, towards the end of his life, Titmuss in *The Gift Relationship* directed attention to the link between institutional forms and private behaviour. But the voluntary system of blood donation he celebrated owed nothing to the recent extension of statutory services. Rather it could be argued that intensifying reliance on, and competition for, statutory resources and interventions, and the growth of articulate interests among the

employees of the state, have been inimical to the values of altruism
and trust embodied in the blood transfusion service.

When one turns away from these broader moral and
philosophical issues to the more specific goals of particular services,
the picture remains discouraging. The evidence from evaluations of
professional interventions in education, health and social work
hardly serves to explain or justify all the resources that have been
devoted to them. A similar scepticism is merited by the great
reorganisations of local government, health and the personal social
services, in which much reforming zeal was invested.

There are therefore strong reasons for questioning the doctrines
and assumptions that have informed the development of the social
services in the 1960s and 1970s. To these must be added the effects
of the oil crisis on the economies of Western Europe, the
consequences of the peculiar, native inadequacies of the British
economy and the results of the recent swing to the right in British
politics. Together these factors suggest that a resumption of the
pattern of development of the past two decades is neither possible
nor desirable. It would be a mistake to try to put the needle back on
the track and let the same record play on. Fresh assumptions and
fresh guiding principles are required, and in particular a reappraisal
of the role of the state in social welfare. It is to these tasks that our
book is addressed.

The economic life of this country is dominated to a degree
unequalled in the non-communist world by a few large enterprises.
Similarly, the social services of this country are exceptionally
centralised and dependent upon provision made directly by the state.
Hence any reappraisal can usefully begin by examining how this
centralisation has come about, and whether there were not
alternatives to the pattern of centralised, statutory dominance. These
questions form the theme of the first part of the book (Chapters 2
and 3).

The second part (Chapters 4–7) examines the present situation as
it has evolved over the past two decades. It seeks to substantiate the
critique outlined above of the limited benefits that have accrued from
the expansion and reorganisation of statutory services, examining in
broad terms each of the five main social services and looking more
closely at certain specific aspects of them. It then reviews the present
extent and role of the voluntary, informal and commercial sectors.
Finally it argues that the social democratic system developed in
Britain in the postwar years has reached a point of crisis.

Our approach is a critical one. But what is being criticised is not the basic idea of making collective provision for social welfare: rather it is the forms by which this provision has come to be made. Some will argue that at a time when the basic idea of collective provision is under attack, any criticism of the social services can only be damaging. Our view is that an essentially defensive strategy has little to commend it since it is likely to inhibit fresh thinking. Only by identifying the limitations of past patterns can the new strategies required to carry forward the development of the social services be evolved.

The third part of the book (Chapters 8–11) points towards alternative strategies of development. The future of the social services is bound up with wider developments in the economy and society. One view of the future, and perhaps the one most widely if tacitly subscribed to today, is that the present crises in the economy and in the role of the state can be overcome and that the growth of the social services can be resumed as before. This is the argument that the needle can be put back on the record at the point where it was recently knocked off. Two other views of the future can readily be identified with the standard prescriptions of the right and of the left. The right argues for a pruning back of the state to allow more play for the market; the left for economic autarky, for a dominant, expanding and *dirigiste* role for the state in the social services as well as in the economy.

Another possibility, and the one sketched out here, is for a pluralist, decentralised and participative pattern of services. This might find expression for the integrative, egalitarian values that informed Titmuss's thinking, without however placing so much reliance upon the state. It would, indeed, compensate for or correct the disbenefits of the economic system, but as much through promoting active involvement in those services as through passive consumption of them. A variety of initiatives and innovations are discussed which point toward forms of service provision that might be more widely adopted. But they are unlikely to make much progress without sympathetic changes in the economy and the political system. The book ends by discussing what those might be.

Not since the Wars of the Roses can the collective self-esteem of the English people have been at such a low ebb as it is today. One response to this crisis of performance and morale is to deplore our apparent failure to measure up to the standards set by other countries, and to see the solution exclusively in terms of resuscitating the economy, so as to return to high rates of growth. Alternatively, it might be argued that, as it has done in response to past challenges, this country should find its own way through the problems of post-industrial society. Following this line of thinking, less emphasis might be given to maximising the gross national product and more to what people do and enjoy that is not defined and measured as economic activity, for example, to work that is not employment, and to technologies that conserve rather than consume. This raises much wider issues. The point is that the questions about the social services pursued in this book should be seen as part of a larger argument about the future of our society. Our contribution to this debate necessarily takes us outside our own fields of specialisation. But the issues at stake require a broad perspective and we make no apology if our approach has more in common with a tract for the times than a scholarly treatise.

CHAPTER 2

The Emergence of the Centralist Faith

Today we are ruled according to the tenets of a centralist faith. The country is governed by a powerful complex of centralised political institutions, and its social services are amongst the most collectivised and bureaucratic in the Western world. Their main features have been determined by national legislation and they are administered by central and local government departments remote from the recipients of the services. A premium is placed on the attainment of standard-quality services over the country as a whole. Autonomous activity by the people, whether the informal care exchanged between family members, friends and neighbours, or the work of formal voluntary bodies, receives little attention in the design of government policies and is poorly integrated with the statutory services.

The system is based on a firm belief that the central government is not only legally responsible for shaping detailed policies for the management of the country but is also best equipped to oversee their administration. Even the present Conservative government, which is committed on paper to reducing the scope of the state, has not been able to resist the temptation to curb the autonomy of the local authorities when it seemed that it was being used to mitigate the effects of central government expenditure cuts.

How has this centralist faith become so firmly established? Its pre-eminence is relatively recent. Indeed, if we look back to the early decades of the last century there is barely a trace of it to be found in either the institutions of government or the ideas of the day. The systems of central and local government then were little more than rudimentary and there were no nationally organised social services. The relief of poverty was the responsibility of the parish. Such provision as there was for schools, hospitals and housing for the poor was mainly organised on a charitable basis. The unit of organisation was typically small and localised, and the quality of relief or service offered often varied sharply from one area to another. Ideological debates of the day centred on the rival merits of local paternalism and *laissez-faire*, not the extension of the role of central government.

For some historians centralist policies are simply the corollary of collectivism, and collectivism is the product of industrialisation. Clearly the major economic, social and political changes that were taking place in the nineteenth century posed new problems which neither the old paternalism nor the new individualism could cope with. Rapid increases in population, urbanisation and the shift from an agricultural economy to an industrial economy, greatly inflated problems of unemployment, poverty, public health, law and order, and led to important shifts in power within the country towards the new middle and working classes. The development of organised public action (or collectivism) to deal with such problems has been a common response in the history of almost all Western countries as they have gone through the phase of industrialisation.

But the history of other industrialising countries by no means bears out the second part of the thesis, to show that collectivism necessarily leads to centralism. In Belgium, Holland and Germany, for example, substantial public funds are devoted to the provision of social services, but within a framework in which independent voluntary organisations play a large role, and in which central control and direction is much less developed than in Britain. Indeed, within this country itself for much of the nineteenth century public services, including what we would now call social services, continued to be run on a local basis by local people. Only towards the end of the century did the centralising process get under way.

In the context of this study it is important to try to understand why Britain came to adopt the centralist path, for it is our thesis that the results of this choice have been detrimental both at the general level to the development of a democratic society, and more specifically to the provision of effective social services. If the centralist system is to be challenged and eventually changed, its origins and nature must first be comprehended.

We suggest that it is useful to approach the analysis of the development of centralism in Britain in terms of three principal themes. First, what we call the predisposing characteristic of the country's history and system of government as it entered the nineteenth century. Next, the interests of the ruling classes and their challengers during the last century and a half. Finally, the momentum created by the growing machinery of centralism itself.

The predisposition to centralism

In contrast to many other Western countries, Britain has a long tradition of powerful central government. For England and Wales this dates back well before the industrial revolution to the dynasty of the Tudors. The English revolution of the mid-seventeenth century saw the end of the strong monarchy but there was only the briefest glimpse of an alternative system of government based on the sovereignty of the people, when the Levellers and their allies made their fumbling and unsuccessful bid for power. After the Interregnum a strong Parliament inherited the right to rule the country. Unchallenged by local parliaments or princes, its power was supreme. It is true that until the nineteenth century the scope of central government was relatively small. Locally, affairs were managed by justices of the peace, by the parish, or the town corporation. But these did not constitute legally autonomous bodies. The ultimate authority in matters of government lay with Parliament. The system of local government was sanctioned by it and could only be altered with its approval. With power firmly entrenched in the national legislature, the country could be said to be predisposed to a centralist response to the emergent crises of industrialisation. Yet at the same time many of the members of the legislature and those they represented were deeply suspicious of the powers of the state, and opposed to extending them. We need to turn to other factors to explain how their reservations and misgivings were overcome, and disbelief or agnosticism was replaced by faith.

The conversion of the ruling classes

Throughout the nineteenth century and for much of the twentieth the central government of Britain has been in the hands of parties representing the interests of property and wealth, joined as time went on by allies from the new professional and managerial classes. For convenience we will refer to this conglomeration of groups and factions as the 'ruling classes'. The use of this shorthand is not meant to obscure the real differences that existed between, say, Tories and Whigs, or Conservatives and Liberals, or indeed within these parties. But it does reflect our view that a common perspective began to emerge between these various interests in their understanding of the role of the state, more particularly in relationship to the development of social policy. It is possible to pick out two main phases in the development of this common approach which brought the ruling classes from a position of implacable hostility to collectivist and centralist policies to a reluctant but firm acceptance of both (Evans, 1978). The first phase can be seen in terms of state intervention to make the world safe for *laissez-faire*, the second as reluctant extension of this intervention in an attempt to ensure the continued hegemony of the right and centre. There was no abrupt break between the two phases. The second begins to be identifiable in the 1870s but only became predominant in the twentieth century. Even then it never completely replaces the first, and the desire to make social policy compatible with the development of free enterprise is still prominent in Conservative and Liberal Party manifestos.

Making the world safe for *laissez-faire*

The Reform Act of 1832 brought into power a new class of industrialists and businessmen who were committed to policies that would create a favourable environment for the full exploitation of the opportunities offered by industrialisation. More of them were Benthamites rather than adherents of Adam Smith. In other words, while they believed that the principles of *laissez-faire* should operate in industry and commerce, they held that the state had a role in creating the conditions to make this possible. Over the following decades a number of targets were identified for state intervention including the Poor Law, local government, public health and law and order. The old system of local parish relief was seen as mollycoddling the labourer, sheltering him from the bracing winds of competition and costing the ratepayer dearly to boot. The Poor Law Amendment Act of 1834 provided the short, sharp shock of the central workhouse, with its scientifically designed deterrent regime in place of the sloppy and costly system of local relief. The following year the reforming hand was turned to local government in towns, and the Municipal Corporations Act swept away many of the bizarre features of their management and substituted a uniform constitution 'based on a model of the best administered municipal corporations' (Chalmers, 1883, p. 72). It was recognised that government intervention was needed not solely to reform the old system but also to cope with new problems thrown up by the process of industrialisation itself. The appalling risks to public health created in the rapidly growing towns and cities of the country were one of the most acute. Faced with dilatory and often ineffectual action by local government, Parliament intervened with its Public Health Act in 1848. Local feet-dragging in the institution of adequate police forces similarly led Parliament to bring in the Police Act in 1856 (Parris, 1969, pp. 230–40).

Out of this and other legislation a new pattern of public services began to emerge. Typically, a central supervisory department was formed which was controlled by the national government. This body appointed inspectors to monitor the local boards which carried out the administration of the service. The local board was elected by ratepayers and was expected to manage its affairs in a business-like, cost-conscious manner, and to submit to rigorous auditing of its accounts. By the 1860s at the centre there was the General Board of Health, the Poor Law Commission, the Home Office (for police and prisons) and a Committee of the Privy Council for education, each with its own system of inspectors and local boards (Midwinter, 1972, p. 207).

For a further two and a half decades the system of local boards flourished, constituting a unique and in many ways promising phase in the history of British local government. The sheer number of different boards, the complexities of the elections involved and the amateurism of many of their members were the subject of criticism and ridicule from the growing ranks of civil servants in the national administration. But as a student of Victorian administration has commented, the boards had their strengths (Midwinter, 1972, pp. 212–13):

In studying local boards of health and small school boards one is sometimes impressed by the recognition of peculiar needs and the deployment of especial responses. Sometimes they were eccentric and amusing but they often appear to have been wholeheartedly searching to adapt national and legislative norms to their own requirements. In some respects, then, they allowed for what now fashionably might be called 'participation'.

It is, perhaps, not too fanciful if we follow this line of thought, to see the opportunity offered by the boards for the development of a highly participative form of local government in which, as the franchise was extended to the working classes, citizens of all occupations would have the chance to become directly involved in the management of services.

However, such developments would not have been regarded as desirable by either those holding power in Parliament or their civil servants. Their plans for local government reform were to abolish most of the boards and replace them, and other institutions of local administration, by new, larger bodies, elected, to be sure, but much more remote in their daily functioning from the life of the citizen.

The reluctant collectivists

The legislation emanating from Parliament between the beginning of the 1830s and the end of the 1860s was principally regulatory and controlling in its content and purpose. In no sense did it provide the basis for a statutory social service. The prudent man was expected to care for himself, the deserving but unfortunate poor were to look to the charity and help of voluntary organisations, the undeserving poor must make do with the barest minimum in the workhouse. Nevertheless, the principle of statutory involvement in the regulation of social and economic affairs of the nation had become firmly established. In the following decades it was to be cautiously extended into new domains in response to the rising challenge of the working classes.

The earliest evidence of this development came soon after the enfranchisement of the town worker in 1867 with the Elementary Education Act of 1870. The provision of basic education for all, made compulsory in other Acts which followed soon after, can, of course, be interpreted simply as an extension of the social control of the state. 'We must educate our masters' was meant to mean, so many argue, 'to know their places'. But there were also other pressures, not least of them increasing foreign competition implying that the country needed a more educated workforce, and demands from the working classes themselves.

The first substantial swing in policy towards an accommodation with the working classes, however, did not take place until the return of the Liberals in 1906. Many of the party members shared Lloyd George's view that the political liberties won by the workers meant little if they were not accompanied by economic security. If political consensus was to be maintained and the new Labour Party was to be kept out of power, then social policy reforms would have to be introduced. The new Liberal government set the pace with its legislation on old age pensions and national insurance for health and unemployment. The First World War gave a new impetus to the drive for accommodation with the working classes (Titmuss, 1958). It was the first total war, fully involving the civilian population. Appeals for their commitment were matched by promises that a better society would be constructed when it was all over. The most immediate and direct consequence of these pledges after the war was government subsidies for private house building and the direct provision of public housing. Subsequently, it affected the whole climate in which social policy developed between the two wars.

It is doubtful if at any time during the interwar period the Conservative or Coalition governments that dominated Parliament had a coherent social policy. Yet it was accepted by successive governments, however reluctantly, that there could be no going back to pre-1914 days and reliance on the unpopular Poor Law to deal with the social casualties. The net result of government responses to the many challenges and crises of the 1920s and 1930s was the evolution of some kind of grudging consensus on the responsibilities of the state in which the right of all citizens to maintenance without the disabilities of pauperism was acknowledged (Gilbert, 1970, p. 308).

But if this policy developed with little sense of a central design, nevertheless almost every measure within it increased the role and power of national government. The growth of intervention in the housing field depended on national legislation and subsidy from the exchequer, responsibility for the unemployed was assumed by a national unemployment assistance board and attempts to revive employment in depressed parts of the country were made through the designation of development areas. The reform of the Poor Law and the vesting of its responsibilities in the local authorities was pursued as an almost personal crusade by the Minister of Health of the day, Neville Chamberlain. The history of this last policy is particularly significant in the context of our study for it illustrates clearly how the struggle between localist and centralist interests can develop and the advantages of the latter. Chamberlain wanted to abolish boards of guardians and pass over control of the Poor Law to the local authorities, not just because of his zeal for order and logic in public affairs, but also because he was deeply mistrustful of locally elected guardians, especially where working-class representatives were predominant. Some working-class boards had started to pay what the government regarded as over-generous rates of relief to unemployed men forced to seek their help. In the end they could only be stopped by the passage of special legislation to tighten control over the Poor Law Unions, but Chamberlain did not hesitate to promote this and ultimately to obtain the transfer of Poor Law responsibilities to the local authorities (Gilbert, 1970, pp. 214–35).

The advent of the Second World War brought almost every facet of public life under the control of the national government. Not only the planning of the conduct of the war but again the need to make commitments for policies in the postwar world led the government to begin to shape new social policies which would accommodate popular demands. Proposals for secondary education for all were embodied in the 1944 Act. A scheme for a national health service after the war was announced. Beveridge was asked to make proposals for the reform of social security.

In the event it was left to the Labour Party to face the challenges and problems of reconstruction but the movement by those on the right and centre towards the provision of a national framework for social policy was clear enough. It had become accepted that the provision of basic social services by the state was a precondition of electoral support.

The choice of the left

The postwar Labour governments have been as wedded to centralist policies as the Establishment governments they succeeded. Indeed, through their programme of reforms they have probably done much more than their predecessors to extend the grip of the national government on the economic and social institutions of the country. Yet in the first four decades of this century it was by no means clear that the party would take this path, for two distinct and incompatible notions of socialism struggled for supremacy within its membership.

Twenty years before the Labour Party was founded a prescient Fabian writer saw the way things would go (Fabian Pamphlet No. 4, 1886, quoted in Ward, 1978, pp. 140–1):

> English socialism is not yet anarchist or collectivist, not yet defined enough in point of policy to be classified. There is a mass of socialistic feeling not yet conscious of itself as socialism. But when the conscious socialists of England discover their position, they also will probably fall into two parties: a collective party supporting a strong central administration and a counterbalancing anarchist party defending individual initiative against that administration.

It turned out very much as he had foreseen, although the state socialists were opposed not so much by anarchists, as by syndicalists seeking to work through unions and the control of the workplace. The state socialists gave primacy in their policies to the socialisation of industry. By this they meant a form of public control which would be exercised by local authorities or through boards controlled by Parliament. No place was planned for representatives of the workers in this system. Behind this strategy lay a number of beliefs. First, that the capitalist system was extremely wasteful and that its replacement by a well-ordered state-run system would rapidly produce substantial gains in the wealth available for distribution to the people. Secondly, a socialist society should be one with much greater equality of income and wealth and this could only be obtained by state intervention. Thirdly, that freedom in a socialist society was about having more leisure to pursue one's personal interests, and had little or nothing to do with what went on in one's workplace. As Philip Snowden, writing for the Independent Labour Party, put it (quoted in Glass, 1966, p. 14):

> The industrial freedom of the workman may be secured by . . . the reduction of the hours of labour in necessary work to the lowest point so as to leave the individual with ample leisure to follow the bent of his own tastes.

A key tenet in the state socialists' faith was their belief in what could be achieved through efficient administration. Most of them probably agreed with the Webbs, those enthusiastic exponents of a socialist bureaucracy, that the potential of nationally directed services had already been proved by example (Webb and Webb, 1963, p. 243):

> Not only in the manufacturing and other civilian departments of the Army but at least equally in the gigantic Post and Telegraph service, together with the Customs and Excise and the Inland Revenue, the whole organisation, both central and local, exhibits no failure in the uniform execution of whatever is prescribed from the top, with results that are anything but inefficient.

There would be nothing undemocratic in the functioning of these efficient machines for they would be run by professionals who would know it was their place to advise, not decide (Webb and Webb, 1923, p. 143):

> The independent professional, whether costing auditor or efficiency engineer, medical man or educational adviser, will report according to his knowledge; but he will give no orders and exercise no authority. His function is exhausted when his report is made . . .

In complete opposition to this view of socialism were the syndicalists, guild socialists and others who supported various forms of industrial democracy. Although differing in many ways, these groups were united in their suspicion of the powerful state and its administrative machine, and in agreement on the centrality of self-management in the workplace in the socialist society. Even if work hours were to be reduced, work would remain a major part of life. It should be fulfilling in itself and the principal means of sharing power in society. How could men and women participate fully in political democracy if they did not have an active role in that part of their public lives which concerned them most directly? And how could the power of the state be kept within bounds unless it could be divided up into small packets, including the self-managed enterprise?

These views were not confined to the theorists. They were alive in the trade unions in the early years of the century; they helped inspire the shop stewards' movement during the First World War; they were embodied in the development of guild socialism during the same period and the years immediately following the war.

When a new constitution was drawn up for the Labour Party in

1918 its wording reflected the unresolved conflict between these two opposing approaches to socialism (Brand, 1965, p. 55). In the section on objectives, the famous Clause IV on the ownership and control of the means of production could accommodate either view:

> To secure for the producers by hand or by brain the full fruits of their industry, and the most equitable distribution thereof that may be possible, upon the basis of the common ownership of the means of production and the best obtainable system of popular administration and control of each industry or service.

During the 1920s and 1930s the struggle between these two camps continued. Direct action to extend workers' power through encroaching control did not prosper in a period of recession and political defeat. By the 1930s the focus of the debate had moved from the issue of workshop control to the role of workers in the direction of the nationalised industries. The left, supported by Bevin and the Transport Workers' Union, wanted direct union representation on the boards that would run the industries. The right, led by Morrison, believed this would undermine the case for making appointments to the boards purely on the basis of ability and capacity, and would lead to inefficiency. The trade union movement was divided. While some unions backed the Transport Workers, others were obviously chary of the consequences of accepting responsibility for management decisions which membership of the boards would imply. However, Morrison could not get his proposals accepted by party conference and the constitution of the boards was left open. It was not until the Second World War, in direct dealings with the TUC over plans for the party programme, that he got his way. It seems that in the final analysis the unions preferred their traditional role of opposition to a new one of co-managers. Wittingly or otherwise they had extinguished the last chances of embodying an element of participative socialism in the postwar settlement. When the Labour manifesto was published in 1945 it contained not a single reference to workers' control (Brand, 1965).

The platform on which Labour was returned to power in 1945 was more or less pure Fabian socialism. The state and its apparatus of administration was to be the instrument of change. Experts would devise and apply a national programme of reform. The public was cast in the role of spectator and consumer, not co-partner. The shape of the new nationalised industries and social services was

determined on grounds of efficiency (sometimes expediency), and
there was no place for shared management with either employees or
users.

The internal momentum of centralisation

The third theme in this sketch of the development of centralism in
British politics is the internal momentum established by the process
itself. Once started, it can be argued, centralism triggers a number of
reinforcing mechanisms which serve to strengthen it and increase
the rate at which it grows.

First, by creating a permanent civil service, centralist policies
establish a category of people whose interests are bound up with the
maintenance and development of the administrative machine. In
simple terms, the bigger the civil service, the greater the career
opportunities, the more the power wielded, the more prestigious the
job. Given this permanence by comparison with the impermanence
of their political masters, civil servants are well placed to influence
policies which affect their interests. Chapman has shown in *Your
Disobedient Servant* (Chapman, 1978) how many factors work
towards the continued expansion of civil service expenditure, what
enormous pressures are brought to bear on anyone who tries to
question seriously the necessity for such increases and instead seeks
to increase efficiency.

Secondly, by concentrating power in the centre and by
implication attracting the best politicians and administrators to work
in national government, a climate is created in which *ipso facto* those
involved in local government are regarded as second rate. This
neatly provides those at the centre with the grounds for recommending still more centralisation.

Thirdly, there are the consequences which flow from the
existence of the centralist machinery itself. Politicians planning new
initiatives must have an eye to what tools are to hand. For example,
a policy that involved giving a key role to the users or employees of
a particular service would have little relevant previous practice to
draw on. Its backers would need to devise not only the reform but
also the means of introducing it. In contrast, a policy that did not
involve any major departure from centralist assumptions would
pose no special problems to the administration and would be likely
to have an easier passage and more certain outcome.

A fourth factor, the question of the time-limit on the office of a government, also relates to this point. Working to a five-year term, governments have to act expeditiously if they are to ensure that their legislative programme reaches the statute book and has some chance of staying there. Developing new methods of administration, which use less centralised systems of management, could well delay the programme. The established centralised system has the advantage not only that it is 'proved' and 'tried' but also that it can achieve quick results.

CHAPTER 3

The Administration of Collectivism

The collectivising and centralising trends described in the last chapter led to the development of new administrative machinery at both national and local government levels. The rudimentary civil service which existed at the beginning of the nineteenth century still relied heavily on patronage, and lacked the expertise and reliability that the introduction and supervision of the new policies required. By the end of the nineteenth century this system had been replaced by a national permanent civil service, based on bureaucratic principles, while in the new local authorities similar administrative developments were taking place on a smaller scale. Today, the complex bureaucracies developed from these beginnings provide the administrative framework of the welfare system. This system is now so taken for granted that contemporary analyses of political and social administration tend to be concerned almost entirely with matters of detail and give little time to examination of the principles on which it is based. However, a study which is attempting to analyse the performance of a key part of this system, and to consider the feasibility of alternatives to it, clearly needs to consider the principles on which it is said to be organised as well as the nature of the more important criticisms which it has generated. This chapter, therefore, begins with a brief sketch of the theoretical underpinnings of our system of political and social administration as it might be presented by an exponent. We then give the critics their turn and review a number of objections advanced against the system.

Administration and the state

The administrative system of government, at least in its formal structure, reflects the source and nature of authority in the political system it serves. Under a representative form of government, where power is concentrated in parliament, what Macpherson has called 'equilibrium democracy' exists. We consider the characteristics of this system more fully in Chapter 7. Essentially, it offers a mechanism for choosing and authorising governments through the competition of two or more parties for power. 'The voters' role is not to decide political issues and then choose representatives who will carry out those decisions: it is rather to choose the men who will do the deciding' (Macpherson, 1977, p. 78). Between elections the government alone is the responsible authority. It necessarily follows that the administrative machine of such a system will be accountable upwards to the parliament (or council, in local politics), and not downwards to the citizen. The governing party requires an administrative machine which is capable of translating its policies into action rapidly and efficiently, and is readily responsive to its directives. These demands have led to the fashioning of administrative institutions which are collectively described as 'bureaucracy'. In popular parlance this term is a pejorative one, immediately conjuring up images of red tape, impersonality and delay. Many academic students of government, on the contrary, have regarded bureaucracy as the most efficient form of administration developed. This does not mean that bureaucratic organisations are infallible, or that the criticisms advanced against them have no foundation in practice. Neither human beings nor their social institutions will ever be perfect. Nevertheless, in relative terms bureaucracy is far superior to any other form of organisation. In the words of its most distinguished student, Max Weber, the choice in modern society 'is only between bureaucracy and dilettantism'.

Bureaucracy

The key features of bureaucracy, from which its efficiency is primarily derived, are hierarchy, specialisation and the methods of selecting and motivating personnel. Authority is vested at the top, typically in a person or group of people appointed from outside the organisation, as for example the minister who heads a government department or the committee in charge of a local authority department. The structure below this apex is designed to allow the specialisation of tasks. A hierarchy of offices and a system of standard rules and procedures unifies the different specialist activities into a coherent whole. Members of the organisation are appointed and promoted on the basis of ability and are expected to perform their duties in a spirit of disinterested public service, free from personal feelings and preferences. Bureaucracies offer, in return for skills, commitment and compliance of their employees, the prospects of a lifelong career in the organisation, good conditions of work including a high level of job security and a pension on retirement, and the *esprit de corps* that can be expected within departments seeking high professional standards and providing high-status employment (Weber, 1948).

Bureaucracy and the professions

Not all the tasks undertaken by public service organisations can be specified with the precision needed to enable them to fit comfortably into the structure of a bureaucracy. Where a substantial element of uncertainty is involved and expert knowledge is needed to cope with the work the problem is solved by recruiting professional staff and allowing them some space within the organisation to exercise discretion. Professional discretion can safely be incorporated in this way, it is argued, because the nature and structure of the professions provide their own safeguards and ensure that it will be used responsibly. Membership of the professions is only achieved after a complex body of knowledge has been mastered and competence proved. Entrance to the profession and conduct while a member are controlled by the membership itself. Not only technical competence but the observance of ethical standards is insisted on.

The role of the professional is particularly important in some aspects of social services work where the problems of individual clients or users are concerned. Needs may differ widely from one person to the next and cannot readily be covered by standard administrative procedures. In consequence, substantial numbers of professionals have been recruited, particularly in the health, education and personal social services fields. Doctors, teachers, social workers and other professionals play a central role in the delivery of these services, and are given a considerable measure of autonomy in the discharge of their duties. Nevertheless, outside their immediate dealings with service users they too must recognise the constraints of the bureaucratic system of which they form a part.

A particular feature of the organisation of the social services is what might be called the client institution. These are organisations such as hospitals, schools, residential homes, and so on, where members of the public receive a service as temporary or permanent inmates. In the early stages of public service reform, in the last century, these institutions were run on bureaucratic principles, strongly influenced by military and factory models of organisation (Midwinter, 1972, pp. 193–4). Today the principles of upward accountability and hierarchical control are still maintained, and the client is still likely to be treated in some respects as a lower-level employee. But purely bureaucratic methods of administration are significantly modified by the employment of professionals in the organisations and the influence of their specialist approaches.

Organisational accountability and reform

All organisations have to adapt from time to time in response to changes in their environments and in the tasks which they are required to undertake. In commercial enterprises the discipline of the profit-and-loss account acts as the primary means for keeping the organisation on course. Public service bureaucracies have no such built-in indicators of their performance but a number of specially created devices and procedures have been adopted to take their place and ensure that the organisation pursues the policies laid down by government and does so in an efficient manner. Internally, the public services have established various performance measures, and are assisted by work study units and a system of audits and annual reports. Externally, the political masters of the services have instituted various systems to make the organisations accountable to them. Foremost of these is the accountability of the minister or committee concerned with a particular service to the elected authority, parliament, or council of which they are part. In most cases, the budget of their service must be approved by the authority and its performance is constantly open to questioning by individual members. In Parliament a more searching form of monitoring the work of central government departments has been introduced with the institution of select committees. These now cover all the major departments and have the right to call for evidence from ministers, civil servants and others on all aspects of the activities undertaken.

Where more fundamental questions are at stake, such as the possibility of a large-scale reorganisation of a department, government can institute a special committee of inquiry or set up a Royal Commission. Finally, individual members of the public are given added protection against maladministration at both central and local government levels, and in the health service, by the appointment of ombudsmen or commissioners to hear their complaints.

The merits of the system

No system of administration has been invented that is without its flaws but the apologists for our present public service institutions would no doubt argue that they are as efficient and effective as one can expect in an imperfect world, and far superior to any previous system. They are accountable to government and readily controlled by it. They offer the basis for the administration of equitable policies, bringing the same benefits to citizens regardless of where they live or what class they belong to. Finally, they are efficient, incorporating as they do tight systems of control and the best use of expert knowledge. It is true that they provide no opportunities for direct public involvement in the management of services but this is not accepted as a criticism since they do not aspire to do so. Administration is a matter for the disinterested expert, not the partisan layman. Direct public involvement would put the principles of both equity and efficiency at risk, and confuse the system of accountability to the elected representatives who control the organisation.

The system criticised

The achievements of this system of administration have been considerable. Through it has been made possible the massive extension of public services which has characterised the first seven decades of the century and which has done so much to change the quality of the ordinary person's life. But in recent years there has been growing evidence of unease about the performance of the public services and in some quarters an increasing tendency to question the fundamental principles on which they are based. It is possible to identify four main themes in these criticisms: non-compliance, inefficiency and ineffectiveness, bureaucratic ossification and the failure to gain the support and involvement of the public.

(1) *Non-compliance*

The theory of bureaucracy assumes, as we have seen, that the administrators in an organisation will carry out the directives of the legally appointed head of the organisation. Their compliance reflects their professional attitude towards their work: policies are determined by political processes outside the bureaucracy and then implemented in as efficient a manner as possible by it. Critics of the existing system argue, however, that such unquestioning compliance cannot be taken for granted. Groups of employees within the bureaucracies, they suggest, have their own interests and pursue them even to the detriment of the official goals of the organisation. This has been well established in studies of industrial bureaucracies (e.g. Gouldner, 1954; Dalton, 1959; Lupton, 1963; Silverman, 1970) and there are no grounds to believe that the same processes do not afflict government bureaucracies (e.g. Blau, 1963; Crozier, 1964). Indeed the latter face additional problems as a result of the typically short periods that political heads of government departments hold office, giving them little time to gain firm control over the permanent civil servants who staff the departments. But the problem of control is by no means confined to this level. Senior officials may in their turn find it difficult to control performance at middle and lower levels of the organisation.

Top civil servants and the minister. The position of the top civil servants in a department, together with their lengthy experience of administration, gives them considerable opportunities to influence their minister and to resist attempts by him to control them. This influence, the critics often claim, is likely to be based on the assumption that the minister is a mere amateur, that the civil service knows best, that it must curb the wilder plans of its political masters and that the future interests of the department must be secured. A number of ex-ministers have claimed to have experienced strong pressures from their civil servants to control them. Richard Crossman, for example, who set out in his first Cabinet post determined to be the boss of his department, described in his *Diaries of a Cabinet Minister* 'the tremendous effort it requires not to be taken over by the Civil Service' (Crossman, 1975, p. 21):

> My Minister's room is like a padded cell, and in certain ways I am like a person who is suddenly certified a lunatic and put safely in to this great, vast room, cut off from real life and surrounded by male and female trained nurses and attendants. When I am in a good mood they occasionally allow an ordinary human being to come and visit me; but they make sure that I behave right, and that the other person behaves right; and they know how to handle me. Of course, they don't behave *quite* like nurses because the Civil Service is profoundly deferential – 'Yes, Minister.' 'No, Minister.' – and combined with this there is a constant preoccupation to ensure that the Minister does what is correct.

Behind these attentions, says Crossman, lies the determination of the department to see that the minister should follow its line. Secret discussion goes on amongst the civil servants on how this end should be achieved (p. 31):

> There is a constant debate as to how the Minister should be advised, or, shall we say, directed and pushed and cajoled into the line required by the Ministry. There is a tremendous esprit de corps in the Ministry and the whole hierarchy is determined to preserve its own policy. Each Ministry has its own departmental policy, and this policy goes on while ministers come and go. And in this world, though the civil servants have a respect for the Minister, they have a much stronger loyalty to the Ministry.

Another ex-minister, Michael Meacher, gave an account of three strategies which he said he had observed during his time in office being used by the civil service to subvert the political control of ministers (Meacher, 1979):

> One is the manipulation of individual Ministers, an exercise in management which is skilfully orchestrated and on which a great deal of time and care is spent. Second is the isolation of Ministers and the resulting dependence on the Whitehall machine, for which a heavy price in policy terms is paid. Third is the exploitation of the inter-departmental framework, in order to

circumvent Ministers who may be opposing the Whitehall consensus.

Criticism is not confined to politicians on the left. A Conservative minister, Michael Heseltine, appointed Secretary of State for the Environment in 1979, and committed to making economies in his department, found that not the least of his difficulties was establishing just how the organisation functioned (Heseltine, 1979):

In May I was told that there were 52,122 people in my Department. How could I know what they all do all day? How could I take decisions, or reach informed judgements, on relative priorities? I have general advice on every policy issue – but no analysis of how each part of the machine operated, why it operated in that way, and how much it cost. I do not know. Nobody knows.

Lacking such rudimentary but essential knowledge, the minister faces major problems in taking firm control of his department (ibid.):

Because political leadership lacks such detailed information it is at the mercy of pressure groups. And the biggest group comprises those administering a department or a local authority. If options are called for, the usual response is to submit the least attractive in political terms, the easiest to achieve in administrative terms, and with the minimum effect on those putting them forward. Because the Minister or councillor does not know what is going on elsewhere, he cannot devise alternatives. If you do not know what people are doing, how much it costs and why they are doing it, how can there be an informed debate?

Further, even when the general direction of policy has been determined by the politicians, considerable influence remains with the civil servants because of the advantages they possess in controlling the detail of preparing and drafting the relevant legislation. In the final analysis, as a recent study of the civil service suggests, much may turn on the relative abilities of the minister and the top civil servants (Kellner and Crowther-Hunt, 1980).

The professionals. The critics have also attacked the performance of many professionals in the public services. They believe that far from being disinterested and neutral in the way they conduct their work, they abuse the discretion allowed them to concentrate on priorities based on professional preferences rather than a balanced assessment of user needs. Doctors, for example, are accused of giving undue attention to acute illness and the more spectacular treatments such as open heart surgery, to the cost of more chronic cases, particularly amongst the elderly. Similarly, social workers are criticised for putting children and families at the top of their client lists when there are so many more disabled, mentally ill and handicapped, and old people requiring their attention. Another line of criticism concerns the use of the machinery for maintaining the standards of the professions and exercising discipline over backsliding members. It is argued that in practice the professions are reluctant to apply sanctions to their own members, and more often tend to close ranks in the face of criticism.

Again, the employment of professionals in client institutions has not provided any guarantee that the organisations will always be well conducted. Bureaucratic structures can sometimes be used to protect staff of low calibre and commitment. In the most extreme cases, mainly where organisations are relatively isolated from contact with the outside world, the inability to establish sound professional standards and to control staff behaviour has been followed by the gross abuse of power, as the revelations about some long-stay institutions have shown (Committees of Inquiry, 1969, 1972; Farleigh Hospital, 1971).

Lower-level employees. Problems of control extend to the lowest levels of the hierarchy. Distance from management often makes it difficult for the administrators to know just how lower-level employees are discharging their duties. This is especially true where the workers are directly involved with members of the public as, for example, in the cases of nurses in the hospital and counter clerks in the social security office, and the decision-makers must rely on their co-operation in arriving at the correct course of action (Stevenson, 1973, pp. 61–3).

Another way in which lower-level employees have acquired increasing influence, it is argued, has been through their involvement in unions and in politics outside their organisations. In the Labour Party these *petits fonctionnaires*, both through their unions such as NALGO, NUPE and ASTMS, and through their individual membership of constituency parties, have come to play a significant role in shaping policy. Unsurprisingly, much of their influence appears to be directed towards maintaining or increasing the strength of the statutory sector.

In summary, the critics of the contemporary system of administration argue that the performance of the public bureaucracies will be substantially influenced by employees at different levels in the organisations and their definitions of *their* own interests. Compliance cannot be assumed but has to be negotiated, often in a covert manner, and this process can lead to a more or less serious deflection of the organisations from the pursuit of their 'official' or politically defined goals.

(2)   *Inefficiency and ineffectiveness*

A second strand in the contemporary criticisms of public administration concerns their efficiency and effectiveness. Efficiency, it is suggested, as defined in terms of cost, is hard to ensure in non-profit-making organisations. How is the performance of the separate units which constitute the organisation to be identified and measured? And how is the individual employee to be made accountable? Current systems of work measurement and internal audit are quite unequal to solving these problems, the critics argue. Indeed, predominant pressures within the system are claimed to encourage profligacy rather than restraint. For example, one former civil servant, Leslie Chapman, who carried out a cost-saving crusade in the Ministry of Works, believes (Chapman, 1978, p. 48):

> Almost every pressure on management in the Civil Service, and probably within the rest of the public sector, is a pressure to spend more and more money. The reason for this is that positive pressures to save can only come from those who would benefit from such savings, that is, the tax payers who have no organised voice.

In Chapman's opinion the roots of the trouble can be traced to the lack of individual accountability, the lack of competition within the service, and immunity from personal consequences in the case of failure which almost complete job security guarantees. These result in an inertia which is at its most pronounced in the higher grades of the civil service. He believes a substantial proportion of the staff at this level oppose change almost on principle (p. 126):

Whenever anything new is proposed they see the possibility of complications and find it necessary to consult numbers of other people of their own kind. Their attitude to all things and especially to proposals for change, and, most of all to proposals for increasing efficiency, is one of mildly amused unconcern. Enthusiasm is vulgar. Certainty about anything is probably irresponsible. They are the products of a system which was designed in the middle of the nineteenth century, and they have no relevance to the conduct of public business today. The salaries they draw are a waste of taxpayers' money and by blocking changes and improvements they cause the waste of immensely greater sums.

Effectiveness, as defined in terms of the achievement of the official goals of the organisation, is also questioned by the critics. Take, for instance, the need of a social services organisation to be responsive to client needs. People at the top of the bureaucracies, with the power to effect changes in the service, are remote from the point of delivery and will often be poorly informed about the practical impact of the organisation's policies. Those at the bottom of the hierarchy, at the point of service delivery, and who are well informed about the effects of their work, have the least power to change the system. Bureaucracy can all too easily become ossified in a particular form and continue to function ineffectively for years before the major intervention from the top which is needed to unfreeze it takes place (Crozier, 1964).

(3)   *Bureaucratic ossification*

Critics of the present system of public administration also tend to have strong reservations about the adequacy of the methods which exist for keeping them on course and reforming their structures as necessary. They are largely mechanistic, and incorporate little or nothing from the research which has been carried out on bureaucracies in recent decades. Two important themes in this work are held to be particularly relevant: alienation and negotiation. The studies of the human relations and neo-human relations schools have shown the alienating character of much routine work in bureaucratic organisations (Argyris, 1957; Friedmann, 1964; Likert, 1967). They have gone on to suggest ways in which the restructuring of jobs to make them larger and more challenging and the active participation of employees in decision-making in the workplace can contribute to the reduction in alienation and an increase in the responsible involvement of workers. Nevertheless, as action researchers have indicated, some basic differences in interest between workers and management are likely to persist (Silverman, 1970). The implication of this must be the frank recognition of such differences and willingness to negotiate openly to establish the basis for compliance in more flexible and adaptive ways of working.

Some major industrial and commercial enterprises have been quick to see the relevance of such policies and have endeavoured to incorporate them in their organisations (Likert, 1967; Paul and Robertson, 1970). But the public bureaucracies, their critics claim, have been very slow to follow suit. When reforms are made they tend to be confined to more traditional scientific management strategies such as PPBS, work study and corporate management. It is difficult to explain the reluctance of the public services to experiment with the more radical strategies except in terms of innate conservatism and inertia, or the belief that any formal invitation to employees to participate in decision-making would be incompatible with the system of authority on which the organisations are built, and would threaten entrenched interests. The public services have a formidable capacity to resist change, the critics argue. Even the recommendations of a Royal Commission can be circumvented when they are found to be disagreeable, as was the case with some of the Fulton proposals (Jones, 1972; Chapman, 1978).

(4)   *Failure to gain public support and involvement*
Representative systems of government in which all power is vested in the elected members of parliament or local authority logically exclude the right of the citizen to participate directly in the management and delivery of public services. Nevertheless, the system implies that people should be able to become involved, at least in the sense that they should have ready access to representatives and officials to make their views known and obtain their rights, and that they should be able to contribute their support for the services through various forms of voluntary action. Critics of the representative system, however, argue that in practice involvement of the former kinds has become increasingly difficult and that the exclusion of citizens from direct participation is particularly costly in terms of resources forgone and the potential for creating more responsive services.

Access to representatives at the local level has been made more difficult as the scale of government has increased. In particular, the reforms of 1974 led to the disappearance of many small units of government, the urban and rural district councils and county boroughs, and replaced them with much larger and more remote authorities. Not only was the number of representatives reduced but the seats of government were moved from many of the smaller towns to places distant from their inhabitants. Councillors had to cover wider areas and to represent more constituents per head. The same centralising process often made contacts with local authority officials and departments more difficult for the citizen as services were concentrated in new districts and county headquarters.

Reforms in the health service have likewise made access more difficult where local authority health functions were absorbed by the NHS and political representation was removed to the area health authorities, bodies remote from the local level.

At the same time administrative rationalisations and new managerial techniques have frequently increased the gap between provider and user and diminished community involvement. Thus, for example, the introduction of the large district general hospital, with the concomitant closure of many small local hospitals, has created problems of access for many people and often dissipated the active voluntary support and feelings of loyalty that the local institutions engendered. Using the instance of the closure of a particular local hospital at Wallingford, Crossman described the process by which the decision to build one such district general hospital (at Reading) led to the closure of a local hopsital at Wallingford despite all the warnings as to its social costs (Crossman, 1976, pp. 269–70):

No one denies the case for the new district hospital. But what I point out to you is that the case for a balanced building programme was not given sufficient importance and so the interests of cure squeezed out the interests of care. The convenience of the consultant was given very high priority; the convenience of the patient and the family who wished to visit him a very low priority.

Similar problems have often been created by the closure of small village primary schools and the bussing of children to larger institutions, sometimes many miles from where they live.

Another aspect of administrative reform has involved increased reliance on modern managerial methods, again often without apparent consideration for their social costs. For example, the abolition in many authorities of weekly rent collection has cut a regular and valued link between tenant and management. It is claimed that its consequences have included more rent arrears, greater vandalism, longer delays in repairs and more tenant alienation.

It is true, of course, that in recent years some statutory social services organisations such as hospitals and local authority social services departments have made increasing efforts to recruit the support of volunteers. Further, consultative committees of various kinds have been introduced, to give the public some voice in the management of services, as in the case of the community health councils. But such developments, the critics claim, are a poor substitute for the institutions and relationships lost through centralisation and rationalisation, and are a thin imitation of truly participative policies. They argue that to maximise the involvement of the citizen in meeting the social needs of the community it is essential to organise the statutory services in such a manner that they can be controlled and delivered locally, allowing strategies to be hammered out at this level between statutory and voluntary interests. 'No participation without direct representation' might be their slogan. They also maintain that direct involvement of this kind by the public would provide the basis for a much more discriminating and effective system of monitoring the performance of statutory services.

Discussion

What is the significance of these criticisms? One view is that while they may take the gloss off the idealised account of the contemporary system of government and administration presented in the first part of the chapter, this is only of limited importance. Infallibility has never been claimed for the system, even by its most enthusiastic advocates. Its peculiar virtue, it is suggested, is that for all its imperfections, it works in practice. The very complexity of modern government and the dramatic improvements in public services that it has made possible stand in evidence.

But from another perspective the implied levels of inefficiency and ineffectiveness are seen as serious causes for concern. This is not only because of the issues of control and use of public resources that are involved but for the doubts they throw on the capacity of the system to cope with the growing crisis now facing the country. Can this system adapt not only to take account of criticisms of its current deficiencies to deal with a situation in which economic growth is no longer assured but in which the demands and pressures placed on collective provision are increasing sharply? And if it cannot, what realistic alternative is there to it? In Chapters 4–7 we consider evidence on these issues by examining key aspects of the recent performance of the state in the social policy field. In Chapters 8–11 we turn to consider the feasibility of an alternative approach, based on a different conception of the role of the state and its administrative machinery.

CHAPTER 4

The Performance of the Statutory Services

Between 1961 and 1976 the proportion of the gross national product (GNP) devoted to the social services rose from 17 to 28 per cent. Over the same period the GNP itself increased in real terms by over 40 per cent. so the social services were getting a growing slice of a growing cake. This chapter asks what the money was spent on, and poses some critical questions about what has been gained thereby.

Starting off with a synoptic view, Table 4.1 shows the rate of growth in expenditure on each of the five main services. Although the personal social services have risen rapidly from small beginnings, they are still much the smallest of the five services in

Table 4.1   *Public expenditure on the social services, 1961–76 (£m.)*

	1961	1971	1976
Education	1,012	2,899	7,300
	100	286	721
Health	930	2,249	6,089
	100	241	655
Personal Social Services	66	310	1,169
	100	470	1,771
Social Security	1,628	4,308	11,237
	100	265	690
Housing	555	1,310	5,084
	100	236	916
Total	4,191	11,016	30,876
	100	264	737
As a proportion of GNP	17·3	22·5	28·2

Sources: National Income and Expenditure 1972, table 49; 1976, table 9.4.

terms of expenditure. The next most rapid expansion has been in housing, which is in part attributable to the large rise in interest rates in the mid–1970s. The other three services have experienced similar rates of increase, with social security remaining in financial terms the largest service.

Education

In the fifteen years under review public expenditure on education increased in real terms just over two times and in relation to the GNP went up from 3·6 to 6·4 per cent. Much of the increase was due to more people being educated. The biggest rise was in the number of full-time students at universities and colleges: there were almost three times as many of them in 1975/6 as in 1960/1. In contrast the number of pupils in schools rose only by 30 per cent, the rise being due partly to the larger numbers born in the early 1960s working their way through the schools, partly to the raising of the school-leaving age and even more to voluntary staying on beyond the school-leaving age (*Statistics of Education 1975*, Vol. 5, table 1). There was also an increase in the number of children under 5 being educated in nursery schools and classes but this accounts for only a small part of the total increase in expenditure. Numbers, however, do not tell the whole story. Another reason for increasing expenditures is changes in unit costs. Broadly speaking, when price changes are discounted, costs per student in further and higher education have remained remarkably constant. In contrast costs in schools increased considerably, particularly at the primary level, and were due more than anything else to reductions in the pupil/teacher ratio (*Statistics of Education 1977*, Vol. 5, table 11). Thus, in seeking to appraise the increase in public expenditure on education, the main questions that need to be asked concern the expansion of full-time education beyond the age of compulsory schooling and the growth of costs in schools.

The expansion of further and higher education means that since the early 1960s the proportion of the relevant age-groups undertaking a period of full-time post-school education has doubled. What has been gained as a result? Many students value higher education essentially for non-material reasons, say, for the opportunity it provides for personal development. Indeed the experience of higher education seems to reinforce non-material, non-instrumental goals. Thus a study carried out more than ten years ago showed that although when students arrived at university the goal of 'qualification and skills' received the most endorsements, after they had been there eighteen months it was displaced as the most widely accepted goal by 'broad education and appreciation of ideas' (Brothers and Hatch, 1970, ch. 11). Hence there are important benefits to be derived from higher education that cannot be measured in pecuniary terms. However, it is not clear that some of these might not be obtained at much less public expense by other kinds of post-school experience.

Higher education also offers benefits of a material and pecuniary kind, since it provides qualifications which enable those receiving them to obtain more desirable, better-paid jobs. From the point of view of an employer a degree may indicate that its holder has skills and knowledge directly relevant to the work for which he is seeking recruits. Medicine is an obvious instance of where this is true. However, in many situations a degree is not of direct relevance to the work to be done. Like other qualifications, it is simply the best single piece of evidence available to employers as to their applicants' general level of ability. In so far as this is true, education performs a sorting and labelling function.

Part of the increase in people with degrees has been taken up by the expansion of occupations for which a degree has for a long time been a necessary qualification. However, occupations such as solicitors, teachers and librarians are now increasingly expecting their entrants to possess a degree. This has two effects: some occupations are becoming closed to people who have not undertaken higher education, and the number of years of higher education required of entrants is increasing. In the case of teaching the norm has risen in recent years from two years to four years. This tendency to demand higher qualifications is particularly marked in the public sector, including especially the social services. The point here is that the expansion of post-school education has to be seen in part as the product of a competitive process for a limited supply of desirable jobs. More time has to be spent and higher qualifications are needed to get the same job. As Hirsch puts it, 'it is a case of everyone in the crowd standing on tiptoe and no one getting a better view' (Hirsch, 1977, p. 49). Thus increasing resources are absorbed simply by competition for what he defined as 'positional goods'. The people who gain higher qualifications may still get better jobs and earn more, but that there is a large public economic benefit from spending more money on higher education is increasingly questionable.

The other side of the coin is the growth of professionalism. An important aspect of professionalism is the restriction of jobs to people with the requisite qualifications. The higher and more specific the qualification barrier, the greater the number of potential employees who will be excluded by it. This is justified on the grounds that a relevant qualification is evidence that its holder has acquired knowledge and skills that are necessary for competent performance. This assumption, on which so much post-school education rests, is largely untested. Although clearly specifiable knowledge and skills are essential for some jobs, it is not evident that the level of a qualification or its class are at all closely related to success in employment.

Thus the House of Commons Committee on Expenditure, reporting the views on postgraduate education of a number of major employers, concluded that a higher degree might serve to identify able people, but had little other value outside the academic world (House of Commons Expenditure Committee, 1974). American evidence on this subject is much less sparse than the British. Reviewing studies published up to 1965, Hoyt concludes that 'College grades have no more than a very modest correlation with adult success no matter how defined' (Hoyt, 1965, p. 45). Writing a few years later Warren found that subsequent research did not invalidate this conclusion. Furthermore, examining numerous studies of the relationship between first degree grades and success in the first year of graduate study, where one might expect to find a closer relationship than anywhere else, he discovered a median correlation of only 0·30 (Warren, 1971).

In addition, particularly in the social services, there are situations where people without qualifications, who have not been through the socialisation process of higher education, may be better able to do certain kinds of work than those who have. This is particularly true where being able to help people depends on the lack of social distance between the helper and the helped, as may be the case with helping the elderly or community work with deprived communities. The creation of barriers to the employment of people like this is the negative aspect of higher education, professionalisation and the social services.

A rather different set of reasons for scepticism about the benefits of the increased resources devoted to formal education emerges from an examination of primary education. Many of the benefits of education cannot readily be measured, but this does not mean that no comparison of inputs and outputs should be attempted. As already indicated, expenditure per child in primary education increased considerably during the later 1960s (*Statistics of Education 1977*, Vol. 5, table 12). This was in real terms. Classes got smaller and the teachers more highly qualified, while there was also a substantial investment in new school buildings. What of the outputs? Quite good measures do exist for one undisputably important output – literacy. Trends in literacy were examined at some length by the Bullock Committee. The committee refuted the more alarmist comments about declining standards, but concluded (Bullock, 1975, para. 2.29) that:

At the age of 11 no significant change in reading standards over the decade 1960–1970 emerges from the NS6 survey. But the movement in Watts-Vernon scores from 1964–1970 just achieves significance (at the 5% level), so that such movement as did occur was in all probability downwards. The indications are that there may now be a growing proportion of poor readers among the children of unskilled and semi-skilled workers. Moreover, the national averages almost certainly mask falling reading standards in areas with severe educational problems.

Thus in terms of improvement in literacy increased resources seem to have made no difference. Subsequently, there has been a continuing increase in per capita expenditure. A report by the DES Inspectorate (DES, 1978) included data which suggested that there had been an improvement in literacy between 1970 and 1977. But this can be attributed to the growing concern for literacy associated with the establishment of the Bullock Committee and the dissemination of its report, and does not contradict the view that what matters is not simply the level of resources, but how they are used.

It is of course important to recognise that the acquisition of basic skills and academic attainments is far from being the only goal which schools pursue, and that modern as compared to traditional practice in schools probably gives greater weight to personal development, creativity, the widening of interests, and so on, and to attainments not readily measured in terms of the results of examinations and tests. But in the absence of evidence that children have become more creative, and that this is due to the availability of more resources and/or at the expense of literacy, the general point emerging from this analysis holds good. This is that the returns on increasing educational expenditure seem to be low.

These conclusions will not be surprising to those familiar with the evidence on class size, pupil/teacher ratios and attainment in schools. The relevant research has been summarised by Rutter and Madge (1976, p. 126) and indicates paradoxically that if anything there appears to be a positive association between larger class size and attainment. In similar, though broader vein the synoptic and influential American study by Jencks (1972) pours much cold water on claims as to the benefits of more investment in schooling. However, recent research in this country by Rutter and his colleagues on secondary schools (Rutter *et al.*, 1978) has shown that schools can vary considerably in their effect on academic attainment, attendance, behaviour in school and delinquency. Moreover, the schools studied tended to do well or badly on all these criteria, rather than well on some criteria and badly on others. Rutter indicates that what is significant is the way schools use their resources and the ethos which the school establishes, rather than the quantity of the resources deployed. Yet policy-makers can much more easily influence the level of resources allocated to schools than what goes on inside them. Hence much recent educational development has been a story of increasing resources being made available as a proxy for changing the way they are used.

Health

Public expenditure on health has increased at a rate similar to that of the other main social services, from 3·8 per cent of GNP in 1961 to 5·6 per cent in 1976. However, it has suffered less than other services from the cuts in public expenditure imposed by the Thatcher government. The pattern of development has not been an even one: the character of it is best indicated by the changes in the number of staff working for the national health service shown in Table 4.2.

It is the hospitals that have attracted the bulk of resources in recent years, in terms of new building as well as of staff. The number of people admitted to hospital has gone up by about a quarter, while the average length of stay has gone down, so that

Table 4.2   *Numbers of staff in national health service, 1959 to 1975,
England and Wales*

	1959	1975	% increase
Hospital staff			
Doctors	16,033	28,450	77
Nurses and midwives	202,306	319,450	58
Professional and technical	21,878	48,684	123
General Practitioners	22,091	23,122	5
Community health nursing staff	c.19,000	33,316	75

Sources: Health and Personal Social Services Statistics, England 1973, table 3.2; England 1976, table 3.2; Wales 1978, table 3.01.

there has been a substantial improvement in the ratio of patients to hospital staff. In contrast the number of GPs has hardly changed, although in the work of primary health care they are now supported by a growing number of health visitors and home nurses.

As with other forms of public expenditure on the social services, it is difficult to argue that the benefit in terms of the health of the public has increased to the same extent as the proportion of GNP devoted to it. The latter has risen by 50 per cent in fifteen years. Apart from substantial, continuing declines in such infectious diseases as tuberculosis, whooping cough and poliomyelitis, the conquest of which resulted from advances made in earlier years, it is difficult to find indicators of improved health that are in any way commensurate to the rise in public expenditure. Thus there has been little change in the numbers absent from work due to sickness or in the numbers claiming sickness and invalidity benefits; and the expectation of life at most ages has not improved by more than about a year.

Over the past century great progress was brought about by improvements in public health, nutrition and mastering infectious diseases, and was translated into a considerable lengthening of the expectation of life. Today progress is more hardly won. Medical advance tends to be epitomised by open heart surgery, which is highly dependent upon newly developed technology and a very expensive way of achieving small prolongations of life.

The high costs alone are one reason for the lower rate of return on additional health expenditure. In addition there is evidence that in some cases new technologies represent little advance on simpler, less expensive methods of health care. A notable instance emerges from a study (Mather *et al.*, 1976) which looked at alternative treatments for people who have had a heart attack: one response is to rush them to an intensive care unit; alternatively they can be cared for at home. The study showed that intensive care did not increase the patient's chance of survival, though it was of course more expensive. Another instance concerns open heart surgery itself. A recent study (Seides *et al.*, 1978) that followed up people who had undergone coronary artery by-pass grafts found that though the operation gave considerable initial relief, five years later in most cases the original symptoms had returned.

The general point is that advanced forms of treatment have a glamour and prestige that more mundane and simpler treatments lack, so that there is a strong temptation for the medical profession to introduce them without a careful weighing-up of costs and benefits. A current case in point is computer tomography (CT). This is an advanced form of body-scanning which makes it possible to identify tumours. It has clear advantages over other methods of diagnosis when applied to the brain, and brain scanners of the new kind have now been introduced in all regions in Britain. But the same cannot yet be said of scanners for other parts of the body, where cheaper methods of diagnosis may be as effective. Moreover, it is not clear that the therapies exist to make use of any advances in diagnosis. Hence a cautious approach would seem to have been called for in introducing the new whole-body CT machines, particularly because they cost (at 1977 prices) ·£250,000 each to acquire and some £50,000 per annum to run. However, the first machines were not introduced in a planned way: enthusiasm for the latest, exciting techniques, the willingness of private philanthropy to provide money for purchasing, though not always running, the machines, and the desire of the manufacturers to establish a home market for the innovation had led by 1978 to the acquisition of the new machines by a handful of hospitals, most of them located in London and the south-east (Stocking and Morrison, 1978). Subsequently they have been introduced more widely as a result of extensive public fund-raising.

CT is a British innovation; and in Britain the organisation of health services, with its emphasis on central control over resource allocation, means that there is more chance of a rational approach to the introduction of new technology than in other developed countries, which spend more on health, where new investment is much more the product of local initiatives by the medical profession and where there is not a sound system of primary care. However, the same trends towards advanced medicine are evident in Britain as elsewhere, even if here they take a less luxuriant form. Increasingly resources are being devoted to highly sophisticated forms of diagnosis and to elaborate types of surgery. The success rate of these is uneven, and the increased expectation of life resulting from them is not always high, added to which the regime required after a transplant may impair the quality of life. No doubt the people with, say, organ transplants prefer to be alive than dead, but seen in a broader perspective, basic questions need to be asked about the priority accorded to acute care. These are raised in a more general form by a paper on 'Health service "input" and mortality "output" in developed countries' (Cochrane *et al.*, 1978). After relating mortality rates in eighteen countries to a number of input indicators such as the level of health expenditure and the number of doctors and nurses, the authors state: 'We believe that one overall conclusion may be drawn from this study. It is that health service factors are relatively unimportant in explaining the differences in mortality between our eighteen developed countries'.

Much ill-health nowadays is caused by diseases and conditions that are not susceptible to treatment on the model of acute care. More prevalent are chronic conditions, often associated with ageing, such as arthritis and strokes, and the bad consequences of styles of living, such as smoking, alcoholic drink, lack of exercise and unbalanced diets. These represent the growing health problems of the future, and it is doubtful if present priorities and structure permit the national health service to respond effectively to them. The effects of preventive measures are notoriously difficult to quantify, particularly ones like health education which are likely to have a broad and diffuse impact. However, there has recently been a decline in the incidence of heart disease in the USA which would appear to be a product of the propaganda in favour of more exercise, better diets and less smoking. As regards more specific measures, Parkes has recently drawn together the results of a number of studies which show the beneficial effects of preventive interventions in reducing psychiatric problems after personal crises, such as being widowed, having a major operation, or being released from prison (Parkes, 1979). But preventive health and health education are generally accorded a low priority; and although in recent years there has been increasing emphasis on community care, especially for the mentally ill and the elderly, this represents only a marginal adjustment rather than a fundamental reappraisal.

Health care can be seen as a continuum stretching upwards from self-care through primary care to secondary, hospital care. The development of medical knowledge, specialisation and professionalisation has pushed care along towards the upper end of the continuum. This puts up costs, means that some people receive more expensive care than they need and in a more general way reduces the returns on additional health expenditure. But perhaps the most important consequence is that it turns the sick person into a passive recipient of medical services, and undervalues the importance for both sick and well people of being active in maintaining their own health.

The personal social services

Although in 1980 the personal social services were subjected to deeper cuts than other services, until recently they were growing very fast from small beginnings. Because of the Seebohm reorganisation which took effect in 1971 and 1972 it is difficult to carry any analysis of changing patterns of provision far back into the past. Hence Table 4.3 relates only to the period 1971–6.

Table 4.3   *Social services departments staff, 1971 to 1976, England*

| | Whole-time equivalents | | |
	1971	1976	% increase
Social workers, including directors, advisers and field staff	10,346	23,985	132
Day and domiciliary staff	41,261	62,054	50
Staff of homes for elderly, disabled and mentally disadvantaged	39,705	54,904	38
Staff of children's homes	17,967*	22,094	23*
Others	15,818	20,905	32
Total	125,097*	183,872	47*

* Data for children's homes refers to 1973, not 1971; this tends to augment the figures for 1971 and hence understate the rate of increase.

Sources: DHSS, *Staff of Local Authority Social Services Departments 1971* and *1976.*

Local authority responsibilities for providing residential care for the elderly, the handicapped, and children were already well established by the time of the Seebohm reorganisation. The table shows that the number of staff employed in residential care has continued to rise, though most of the increase must be attributed to improved levels of staffing, since the rise in the number of residents has been in the order of no more than 10 per cent, which is less than one-third of the rise in staff numbers.

Staff employed in giving day and domiciliary care, a majority of whom are accounted for by the home help service, have increased at a rather faster rate. This represents the emphasis currently being accorded to community care. The largest increase, however, has been in the number of social workers. This rapid growth is partly due to the transfer of medical social workers from the hospitals to the social services departments (SSDs) during this period, and it should be recognised that even by 1976 the social workers amounted to no more than one in eight of all SSD staff. Nevertheless, more than anything else, this growth is a concrete expression of the enlarged 'family-based and community-orientated' role for the personal social services advocated by the Seebohm Report. The extent to which social workers have become a pervasive element in the overall pattern of social service provision varies considerably from area to area, reflecting differing levels of local authority provision.

Thus in the London boroughs with the highest levels of staffing the number of social workers per 1,000 population is about 1·5, compared to figures under 0·5 in most of the shire counties. Nevertheless, despite the wide variations in levels of provision, the capacity of the SSDs to take a broad view of the needs of their area has increased greatly, as the Seebohm Report hoped it would, and the demands and expectations directed at them have risen no less quickly.

However, the character of this development has in significant ways been different from that in education and more particularly health, where much of the growth has been taken up by the extension of the more advanced types of professional service. In the personal social services the professionals have also been advancing their claims, and there has been an emphasis on raising the level of qualifications. In the process of expansion ideas about what social work is or should be have become increasingly confused. In the past social work was to a large extent identified as casework, or at any rate casework was seen as the professional core of social work and the basis of the profession's claim to special knowledge and skills.

This is still the received doctrine in most social work training. Whatever validity these claims may have had, and they have not gone uncontested, today only a small proportion of social workers' clients receive what can be described as casework, in the sense of a continuing personal relationship aimed at helping people with problems (Goldberg and Warburton, 1979, pp. 125–6). Thus in contrast to the situation in health and the upper end of the educational system, in the personal social services the more rarified aspects of professionalism have been diluted by pressing demands for practical advice and services.

One can in fact identify two directions of change, represented in different degrees among different social services. While one direction has been towards the development of larger, more advanced social services institutions, promoting the growth of and providing vehicles for more sophisticated professional skills, there has been another equally significant development. Although sometimes obscured by aspirations towards professionalisation, this is in essence the assumption by the state of increasing responsibilities for the provision of everyday caring: that is, for practical help rather than for the more arcane forms of professional skill. Thus in the five years following the 1971 reorganisation the home help service was extended to nearly 50 per cent more people, and the meals on wheels service to 60 per cent more, the number of children in residential care increased by 14 per cent and the number of places in local authority homes for the elderly by 9 per cent.

One of the reasons for this is changing patterns of family and household living. While in some ways it may be true that the family is changing rather than declining, and that the motor car and the telephone make it easier for members of the extended family to keep in touch and help each other, fissiparous tendencies in actual living arrangements seem to be advancing with surprising rapidity. These are examined more fully in Chapter 6 below. They constitute one of the reasons for the substantial transfer of functions that is taking place from the family to the state, with many women being paid by the state to carry out caring activities not very different from those they might previously have given freely in their own households and communities. The personal social services have been the main recipients of the demands arising from this process, but primary health care and nursery and primary education have also been much affected by it.

These developments raise fundamental questions about the role of the state. On one view of the way the state should respond to these trends it is possible to envisage the state steadily increasing its responsibilities, as fast as growing demand can be translated into decisions to make more resources available. This begs questions about how quickly it will be possible to attract resources, particularly if the prospects for economic growth are poor. It also points towards a society of atomised individuals increasingly dependent on an all-encompassing state. Another view of the future emerges in some of the aspirations expressed in the Seebohm Report for community development and the promotion of reciprocal relationships and mutual aid within the community.

But how far have the new SSDs actually sought to translate these aspirations into action? Numbers of staff now have the word community in the designation of their jobs; increasing use is being made of volunteers, though usually in an essentially marginal role; and here and there area teams are actively pursuing different varieties of what can be described as a community approach. But the main emphasis and most of the growth has been devoted to meeting individual needs through individualised services, to what might be described as a client-centred approach. The level of demand, or what is often described as bombardment, has risen rapidly and tends to exceed the capacities of most area teams. One way of responding to this bombardment is to retreat behind the 'fortifications' of the area office, and offer a carefully rationed one-to-one service. But though this is the usual answer, it is not the only one. An alternative strategy is discussed in Chapter 9.

Social security

Social security has a place in the present discussion on account of the large share of public expenditure on the social services absorbed by it. Thus it amounted to 6·7 per cent of GNP in 1961 and 10·2 per cent in 1976. The increase is attributable to two factors – a growth in the number of people receiving benefits and an improvement in the level of benefits in relation to average earnings. The growth in beneficiaries is in turn mainly attributable to rises in the number of pensioners and of unemployed people. New benefits have also been introduced, notably the attendance allowance.

However, social security is not a service in the sense of the social services so far discussed, since what it provides is money, not help or care from another person. In so doing it constitutes a crucial framework or condition for more personal kinds of helping, whether from statutory, voluntary, or informal sources. But it is the latter, not the former, that are our main concern in this book. Hence there is no need for an extensive discussion of social security here, except to raise the question of how far social security does or does not reinforce other forms of caring. One interesting effect of the introduction of old age pensions by Lloyd George seems to have been a marked reduction in the proportion of elderly people in workhouses (Moroney, 1976, pp. 46–7): families were apparently more willing to care for their elderly members when this did not at the same time involve a drain on their financial resources. The attendance allowance is a recently introduced benefit which will make it easier for a family to care for a handicapped member. But apart from the home care allowance suggested in the Meade Report (Meade, 1978), not much attention has been given to the relationship between financial factors and informal caring arrangements, or to ways of encouraging informal care through either social security or tax allowances.

Housing

Local authorities build houses to let, manage and maintain those houses and subsidise some rents. Central government subsidises the activities of the local authorities, supports through the Housing Corporation a recently enlarged voluntary sector and gives tax relief to house purchasers. It also subsidises rents through supplementary benefits. The extent of the local authority element in this activity can be gauged from the size of the combined local authority housing revenue accounts: these rose from £275m. in 1961/2 to £2,356m. in 1976/7. In addition, in 1976/7 tax relief on mortgages amounted to £1,240m. (UK) and government support for housing associations via the Housing Corporation to £287m.

It is widely held that housing finance is in a mess: that is, the substantial government expenditure on housing is not closely related to clear policy objectives. The main beneficiaries of government expenditure are council tenants and people buying their own houses on a mortgage. On average these benefited to the extent of £210 and £205 respectively per household in 1976/7. The main effect of these subsidies was simply to reduce the cost of housing, but with little reference to anything that might be described as housing need or to the circumstances of the people so benefiting. In addition, poorer families were helped with their housing costs by rent and rate rebates, rent allowances and supplementary benefits. The worst housing is still to be found in the private sector, and private tenants gained little from government intervention except in so far as they benefited from rent allowances and rent controls or were eligible for supplementary benefits.

The British population is well housed in comparison with other European countries (Department of the Environment, 1977, Annex B, table 1), and this is an important and favourable reflection on postwar housing policies. However, expenditure on these policies has been rising, partly because of higher housing costs, especially those arising from the rate of interest, and partly because the two main categories of beneficiaries − council tenants and house purchasers − have continued to rise in numbers. Indeed, they constitute strong vested interests that lie in the path of any reform. The consequence is that although these policies continue to produce a benefit in terms of cheaper housing for a substantial proportion of the population, the rate of return in terms of other goals is declining.

During the 1960s the proportion of GNP represented by public expenditure on housing rose only from 2·3 per cent to 2·7 per cent, but in 1972 it began to rise sharply, reaching 4·6 per cent in 1976. This does not include tax relief on mortgages, which in real terms nearly doubled in the early 1970s. But this growth had only a small effect on the rate at which housing objectives were being achieved. In *Housing Policy: A Consultative Document* (DOE, 1977) the government argued that: 'The traditional aim of a decent home for all families at a price within their means must remain our primary objective' (para. 2.16). But as Table 4.4 indicates, the rate at which the number of households not in decent homes was being reduced altered only a little between the 1960s and the early 1970s. Although this is a highly condensed summary of a complex situation, it does seem that the phenomenon of declining returns on increasing public expenditure applies to housing as well as to the other fields already discussed.

Another major element of public provision is the management and maintenance of council housing. From the point of view of the present discussion, the significant feature of recent developments is the growing interest in a more active role for tenants. One symptom of this is the review carried out by the National Consumer Council

Table 4.4   *Households in unsatisfactory housing, 1961–76, England and Wales (thousands)*

	1961	1971	1976	Annual change 1961–71	1971–76
In unfit or substandard homes	4,700	2,846	1,700	− 185	− 229
In overcrowded conditions	415	226	150	− 19	− 15
Sharing (including concealed households)	1,732	1,246	1,000	− 49	− 49

Source: DOE, 1977, Annex 2, table 4.

(1979) as a result of a request by the Department of Prices and Consumer Protection to consider 'the desirability of the scope for the greater involvement of tenants in the repair, maintenance and improvement of council housing'. A further symptom is the decision of the government to give statutory recognition to tenants' rights.

The growth of interest in tenant involvement is largely a phenomenon of the 1970s. The reasons for it are difficult to pin down authoritatively. Partly it seems to be a response to a general climate of opinion favouring participation, finding expression in the housing field in the spread of tenants' associations. These occur most frequently in authorities with a large housing stock, so that local government reorganisation which substantially increased the size of local authorities may also have added an impetus to the trend. Beyond this the emergence in the 1970s of 'hard to let' estates and problems of vandalism have pointed towards tenant involvement and more responsive management as conditions for the success of public housing.

An active role for tenants can take two forms − one is DIY maintenance and improvement on a personal basis and the other is schemes through which tenants collectively are given a voice in decision-making. The NCC survey found that a quarter of council tenants had carried out repairs themselves in the preceding twelve months, and among those who reported how much they had spent the average sum was £86. Arrangements for giving tenants a say were surveyed by Ann Richardson in 1975, who discovered that a majority of London boroughs and over a quarter of the metropolitan districts had a formal scheme, but that these were rare elsewhere.

Most of the schemes were of recent origin, only a few dating from before 1970.

Altogether, therefore, for both ideological and practical reasons the tacit assumption prevalent in earlier years that tenants should be treated as passive consumers of benevolently provided services may now be on the wane. As the National Consumer Council pointed out, this does not mean that all tenants are eager or able to take on greater responsibilities: but there is a lot of scope for extending the opportunities for further tenant involvement.

A third aspect of the public sector is the construction of houses to let. The design of council housing has been the work of architects employed by or on contract to local authorities. As compared to the private construction of houses for sale, it has for the most part been carried out on a larger scale and according to different canons. Whereas the building of houses for sale has been governed by what the customer could be persuaded to buy and the building societies to lend on, the design of public housing has been subject to cost controls and design standards promulgated by central government, and beyond that the plans have had to be approved by elected councillors. As a result council housing has differed sharply in design and appearance from private housing, even when the private housing has been built at no greater cost.

These differences were never more conspicuous than in the 1960s when much council housing was high-rise and/or system-built. High-rise council housing in Britain began in the 1950s. During the mid-1960s flats in blocks of five storeys or more for a brief period exceeded a quarter of all housing being built by local authorities, and those in blocks of fifteen storeys or more for a short time amounted to 10 per cent. For the most part this kind of building was confined to large urban areas, so that an analysis looking only at the big cities would show an even more marked trend towards high-rise. By 1970 about a million people had been housed in high-rise flats, but new building of this kind had almost come to an end. What was the explanation for its rapid rise and fall?

At a superficial level the fashion might be interpreted as the product of a particular enthusiasm, even megalomania, in the architectural profession, terminated by the collapse of the Ronan Point tower block in 1968. In fact there is a good deal more to the story. Nevertheless, the case of high-rise housing and the associated system of industrialised building is an instructive one for anyone interested in the role of professionals in the public service and more generally in the course of innovations. In addition an interesting though little-known study is available (Cooney, 1974), which is the main source of the account that follows.

A significant part of the impetus behind high-rise lay in the ideas prevalent among the architects who came to the fore in the years after the war. These owed a lot to 'the modern movement' which drew much of its inspiration from Le Corbusier and Gropius. Le Corbusier, in particular, presented a dramatic image of the city of the future, which he described as the Radiant City in the 1920s (quoted in Jacobs, 1975, p. 31):

> Suppose we are entering the city by way of the Great Park . . . our fast car takes the special elevated motor track between the majestic skyscrapers: as we approach nearer, there is seen a repetition against the sky of the twenty-four skyscrapers; to our left and right on the outskirts of each particular area are the municipal and administrative buildings; and enclosing the space are the museums and university buildings. The whole city is a Park.

Here was a vision which cast the architect and the planner in central roles in shaping the forces of technological change, indeed in creating the society that was to come.

Some three decades later there began to loom out of the trees beside Richmond Park a number of tall, grey shapes. These incarnations of Le Corbusier's vision were the work of the LCC Architects' Department. As a report to the LCC Town Planning Committee later explained (*RIBA Journal*, June 1956, p. 351):

> The advantages of high blocks may be summarised as follows; they make possible open layouts with green open space and the maximum public use of the ground; good lighting; good views from the upper storeys; good air; freedom from noise; architectural interest and a contribution to London's skyline, if well sited; in residential areas high blocks of flats give a high density for a small site and make possible a mixed development of the whole area with a higher proportion of lower dwellings with gardens.

Aesthetic considerations thus weighed strongly in the LCC's adoption of high-rise. But there were also non-aesthetic considerations in the claims that high-rise permitted greater densities and more dwellings with gardens. In fact the proportion of dwellings with gardens was never much more than a quarter, even in the original developments which were the model for much that followed. And subsequently many tower blocks were built on far less favourable sites, sometimes as part of developments without any gardens at all. Faced with a shortage of land and strong demand for rehousing people out of high-density slums, high-rise seemed to be the answer. Support for higher densities came also from central government which was concerned to limit urban sprawl and preserve green belts. Thus from 1956 onwards additional subsidies were made available to offset the greater costs of high-rise building. It was hoped that the much greater costs might be reduced by improvements in technology, such as system building seemed to offer. And by the time the 1964 Labour government came to power high-rise and system building together seemed to be the instruments for an ambitious assault on the country's housing problems. Crossman's *Diaries* provide vivid illustrations of government thinking (Crossman, 1975, p. 144):

I am pretty clear what the long-term plan should be. I am pretty clear that the decision means comprehensive urban renewal. We have to concentrate on six or seven places, Liverpool, Manchester, Birmingham, Glasgow, London, where the problem of housing is so bad that the local authorities simply can't grapple with the job ... a Labour minister should impose central leadership, large-scale State intervention, in these blighted areas of cities (November 2, 1964).

Then a little later (pp. 81, 131):

Why shouldn't we assume that instead of doing one little bit of the centre of Oldham we should use the whole 300 acres and have a real demonstration that our system building can work and really does reduce costs? Let's see that one piece of central redevelopment is really finished by us (December 3). . . . in describing my visit to Oldham in this diary I tried to indicate how important industrialised building is to us. Since I wrote that, the Prime Minister has committed us to industrialised building and I see nothing to lose if we make the local authorities turn over to it, since conventional architecture is so terrible it couldn't be worse (January 15, 1965).

But his enthusiasm was not unambiguous, or perhaps it was tempered by further experience. Thus, apropos of Welwyn (p. 159):

> I find it charming and I'm sure it is a delightful place to live in. The Dame, of course, is contemptuous. She loves Cumbernauld. I also like Cumbernauld as architecture, but I feel that the vast majority of British people would probably prefer to live in Welwyn with its red bricks and its North Oxford lilac (February 17).

And of Skelmersdale (p. 173):

> I was very impressed and greatly looking forward to seeing the first new houses they had built since I knew Hugh Wilson, our architect at the Ministry, had done them. Alas, they seemed ghastly to me, like back ends of factories, and they didn't recommend themselves any more when the architect said 'I tried to get the strength and the sheer character of Lancashire' (February 27).

Crossman's enthusiasm for modern architecture for working-class housing thus seems to have been waning before he left the Ministry of Housing. However, it was another two years before a continuation of negative public feeling, particularly with respect to the fate of children in high-rise blocks, growing concern about the extra cost of building high and the Ronan Point disaster of May 1968 made it inescapably clear that this excursion of the professionals into technological innovation was inappropriate.

A general appraisal

The argument advanced so far has been mainly in terms of the specific objectives of the five main social services. The evidence presented has suggested that substantial increases in expenditure have brought only small gains in terms of those objectives. There are also broader considerations against which development can be judged. One which has figured prominently in postwar discussions of social policy is equality, particularly economic equality.

A considerable amount of evidence about trends in the

distribution of income and the redistributive effects of taxes, benefits and social services has become available from detailed analyses carried out by Leonard Nicholson of data collected in the Family Expenditure Survey (Nicholson, forthcoming). This authoritative study shows that in terms of pre-tax incomes the shares of both the top 20 per cent and of the bottom 20 per cent declined a little between 1961 and 1976, that is, those in the middle ranges gained at the expense of those nearer the extremes. In both years the effect of the state in redistributing resources was substantial, but the extent of this effect did not change very much. Putting it more precisely, the redistributive effects of taxes and benefits on the top 20 per cent of households was unaltered, though the bottom 20 per cent gained rather more than they previously did from redistribution (Nicholson, forthcoming, table 5.2). Thus the great increase in public expenditure on the social services made relatively little difference to the extent of inequality.

In part this is because the combined net effect of direct and indirect taxes is small. The main redistributive effect on vertical inequality (i.e. from rich to poor) is brought about by social security benefits, particularly pensions. Expenditures on health and education, taken together, seem to have little effect on vertical inequality; but by benefiting larger more than smaller families they do bring about a significant horizontal redistribution, that is, between households of different sizes and types (Nicholson, forthcoming, tables 4.7 and 4.8).

But there are other dimensions to equality besides the economic: following Max Weber these are conventionally identified as those of status and power. In so far as it is possible to give a clear meaning to equality of status, it is this that is perhaps most directly augmented by the public provision of social services. The allocation of resources by bureaucracies is carried out on impersonal criteria, related to need rather than to social status or wealth. This approach has the virtues of a queue over an auction, and of rights over charity. Thus as more needs have come to be met by statutory services, there have been definite gains in terms of equality of status. Herein perhaps is a clue to the dynamics behind what has been happening.

Questions about the distribution of power in relation to the social services seem to be most appropriately posed by asking how far actual and possible beneficiaries of services can influence the character of those services. These relate to the way the services are organised and to the political systems to which they are accountable, subjects which are discussed in Chapters 5 and 7. Suffice it to say here that the reorganisations of the statutory services have made decision-making more remote from the ordinary consumer. But in response to this tendency efforts have been made to strengthen the voice of the consumer, through such devices as tenants' associations, placing parents on the managing bodies of schools and the establishment of community health councils; while the spread of community action in its many forms indicates that the consumers of public services are becoming more articulate. However, it would appear that these developments are more by way of reactions to the lack of popular control, rather than expressions of effective participation in decision-making. The provision of more services by authorities ultimately subject to the sanction of the ballot box has not done much to make those services responsive to their intended beneficiaries or to redistribute power more widely.

Liberty and fraternity, as well as equality, are other general criteria for judging the social services, but ones which are difficult to operationalise. In a general sense freedom from want is of course a prerequisite for the exercise of freedom to choose. But more specific issues can be raised by asking what choices individuals are actually able to exercise. Choices most obviously exist within further and higher education – between both courses and institutions – and these choices have been greatly extended by the expansion of post-school education. But in primary and secondary education, in health, in housing and in the personal social services the opportunities for choice are more limited: indeed, allocation rather than choice is the more appropriate term for describing how people come to receive one service or facility rather than another. As already argued in relation to equality of power, there has been a growing recognition of the desirability of responsiveness to consumers: but it is difficult to find evidence of anything beyond marginal changes resulting from this. A substantial increase in freedom would come about by extending the private sector and improving the terms on which individuals can opt out of statutory services; but this would be at the expense of equality.

Fraternity can be given various meanings. Interpreted widely, it embraces unilateral, impersonal gift-giving, as of blood through the transfusion service, as well as collaborative relationships between people regarding themselves as equals. Both kinds of activity can be valued for themselves as well as for their contribution to social cohesion and solidarity. It is difficult to envisage fraternity being as direct and explicit a goal of social policy as equality. Nevertheless, the way in which policies are designed can either encourage it or discourage it. There is little by way of fraternity in the supplementary benefits office, or in the usual doctor's waiting room or in the way that local authorities allocate their housing. In essence, services that follow the normal bureaucratic pattern of dealing with individuals in isolation from each other are inimical to fraternity, and much of the expansion of the social services during the past two decades has taken this character. It is voluntary associations that are the natural vehicle for co-operative activity, and only with the encouragement of community development and volunteering during the 1970s have official policy-makers begun to show signs that fraternity has any place in their thinking.

Conclusions

This chapter has argued, in terms of both the specific goals of particular services and of broader criteria, that the growth of statutory services in the past two decades has brought only limited returns. Why is this? There is one, in effect, technical factor which goes a little way towards explaining the lack of achievement. The social services do not show gains in productivity equivalent to those achieved in other parts of the economy; but those who staff them nevertheless have to share in the improvements in the standard of living enjoyed by the population as a whole. More concretely, whereas the productivity of workers in manufacturing industry can be greatly increased by investment in new machinery, equivalent gains cannot be made in most of the social services where direct personal contact between staff and the recipients of services constitutes the essence of the service. Consequently, the real cost of social services is likely to rise in relation to other goods and services. However, as indicated above, the expansion of the social services has involved substantial increases in the volume of services provided, over and above increases in unit costs.

More generally it can be argued that it is unrealistic to expect too much of the social services. Thus the extent to which a society meets such broad criteria as liberty, equality and fraternity reflects structural features of that society which cannot be altered by the social services. Nevertheless they now absorb a large proportion of

GNP and, whether the criteria with which one is concerned are broad or specific, it seems important to pursue further why they apparently produce such limited benefits. This question is the theme behind the chapters that follow.

CHAPTER 5

Reorganisation: Three Case Studies

In Chapter 4 we have given some indication of the low return which has resulted from increased expenditure in recent years in several fields of social policy. So far, however, we have not made a sustained explanation of the kind of thinking which has led to the introduction of these policies and their administration. A major element in our critique concerns the failure of central and local government to develop policies which recognise the existing importance and future potential of the voluntary and informal sectors. This theme is dealt with in the following chapter. Here we are concerned to examine more closely the assumptions which lie behind statutory services and the ways in which they are developed into policies. Our method is to consider recent reforms in three separate but related areas: the health service, the personal social services and local government. The process of devising and carrying through major changes in an area of government provides a particularly good opportunity to identify the basic assumptions of those involved, for it forces what is usually taken for granted and implicit to be made explicit.

In the 1960s and early 1970s national government indulged in a spree of inquiries and reforms aimed at achieving large-scale reforms in the social services and local government. Amongst the most important of these initiatives were the establishment of committees to look at the management of local government and the personal social services, a Royal Commission to recommend reform of the organisation of local government and proposals for the integration of the separate sections of the NHS. Why was there this spate of activity? What provided the impetus for the inquiries? And what was it hoped to achieve? There is very little to suggest that the

public, as users of the institutions concerned, were an important
source of pressure for change. Such evidence as exists of general
public attitudes implies either satisfaction (particularly with the
health services) or indifference (especially as regards local
government) (Draper, 1976; Maud, 1967). However, within each of
the fields concerned there were indications that at least some of the
professionals and administrators running the services favoured
radical changes. The shape of the social services had been
determined fifteen to twenty years previously and some felt it was
high time to make major modifications in the light of accumulating
experience and changed circumstances. As to local government,
current structures had been little modified since the end of the
nineteenth century. Nevertheless, it remains open to question
whether pressures from these sources would have been sufficient to
precipitate inquiries with the power to consider sweeping changes
had a Labour government not been returned to power in 1964. After
thirteen years out of office the party seemed determined to
inaugurate a new era in British politics. With the stirring example
before them of the reforms achieved by the 1945–51 Labour
government, the new government planned further far-reaching
changes in society. Like its predecessor, it believed that such changes
must be planned and introduced centrally.

Reorganisation in local government

The 1960s provide two opportunities in the field of local government
reform to examine the process of planning and implementing
change, and the underlying perceptions and beliefs of those
responsible. The first is offered by the Committee on the
Management of Local Government (1964–7) and the second by the
Royal Commission on Local Government (1966–9). Both inquiries
were chaired by the same man, Sir John Maud, later Lord Redcliffe-
Maud.

The formal task of the Committee on the Management of Local
Government was to consider how local government might 'continue
to attract and retain people (both elected representatives and
principal officers) of the calibre necessary to ensure its maximum
effectiveness'. This might sound like the brief for a rather narrow
inquiry into personnel management and organisational psychology,
but the terms of reference were in effect taken from the title of the

committee and the inquiry ranged over the whole field of management organisation, the relations between local and central government and the attitudes of the public to local authorities, as well as considering staff and elected members.

The Royal Commission had the wider task of considering the whole structure of local government in relation to its existing functions and 'to make recommendations for authorities and boundaries, and for functions and their division having regard to the size and character of areas in which these can be most effectively exercised and the need to sustain a viable system of local democracy' (Redcliffe-Maud, 1969, p. iii).

Why was reform needed?

There was a growing opinion in the 1950s and early 1960s that local government was inefficient. This view could be found not only amongst those in central government, but in academic departments concerned with public administration, and even in the local authorities themselves. Much of the trouble, it was claimed, stemmed from the failure to modify a system that had been developed to cope with conditions at the end of the nineteenth century. Management was adversely affected in particular by the fragmentation of administration through over-powerful and insufficiently co-ordinated committees, and by the prevalence of incrementalist as opposed to innovative policies. Furthermore the boundaries and functions of many local authorities were no longer relevant. In particular there were too many small authorities which could neither attract staff of calibre nor benefit from economies of scale and specialisation.

It is curious to find, however, that when the then available evidence for those opinions about the defects of local government is examined that there were virtually no objective research data to support them. This is not to say that local government was necessarily efficient, but the views that it was inefficient were nothing more than an untested orthodoxy. Nevertheless, lack of evidence, it would seem, need not inhibit the holding of convictions, nor prevent these convictions – when held widely enough, by the right sort of people – from providing the spring for action.

But what triggered the spring? In the case of the Management of Local Government Committee the local authority associations made direct representation to the Ministry of Housing and Local Government to establish the committee (Thornhill, 1971, p. 26). In the case of the Royal Commission it would seem that something as idiosyncratic as the personal feelings of the then Housing Minister, Richard Crossman, and the holiday plans of his permanent secretary, go a long way to explaining its creation.

Crossman found that amongst his most onerous and unsatisfying chores at the Ministry of Housing and Local Government was settling boundary disputes between counties and county boroughs, brought to him by the Boundary Commission. This body had been established in 1958 and was slowly and laboriously reviewing all major local authority boundaries in England. Crossman foresaw a virtually endless stream of cases coming to his desk for adjudication. Keeping the Boundary Commission on would mean 'accepting the war between the county councils and the county borough authorities as endemic in our national life, something I find one of the most stultifying things in our whole governmental system' (Crossman, 1975, p. 65). Some time later he was due to speak to the Association of Municipal Corporations' annual conference at Torquay (p. 331):

. . . I suddenly decided I would add a third topic, the reform of local government and I would announce that the situation was now getting unworkable and I was thinking of winding up the Local Government Boundary Commission . . . I came to the conclusion that I should propose a committee of inquiry with very great authority and with terms of reference that instructed it to lay down the principles of local government reform . . .

This was a spur of the moment decision, and one that he thought his permanent secretary would have squashed, had she not been away on holiday at the time. A year later, reviewing his achievements at the ministry, he picks out the establishment of the Royal Commission as one of his greatest successes (pp. 621–2):

. . . I think I can claim that it was my policy of personal intervention in the decisions of the Local Government Boundary Commission which changed the whole situation . . . In my speech I began to break down the simple notion of the urban area on the one side and the county area on the other and to build up the idea of the city region, the urban area with the rural area attached to it for planning purposes. I launched this idea and simultaneously I denounced the present boroughs and county councils as dinosaurs belonging to a prehistoric age and got a standing ovation for the denunciation.

Of course, Crossman would have had little chance of getting an inquiry going if there had not been a widely held orthodoxy that something was wrong. His standing ovation from the AMC showed something of the support in the cities for his position. The Prime Minister liked the idea too and the proposal had a modernising ring to it which was attractive to a party preparing for an election.

The inquiries at work
Both the Committee on the Management of Local Government and the Royal Commission adopted the usual procedures of such inquiries. They called for written evidence, heard oral evidence, commissioned research and visited some of the institutions in the fields they were investigating. But neither body made any serious attempt to examine and test the basic assumption that something was badly wrong with the prevailing system of local government. That assumption was simply taken for granted.

The Committee on the Management of Local Government proceeded largely by assertion backed up with anecdotal evidence. While the committee was clearly concerned with efficiency it nowhere attempted to define what the term meant. The nearest it got was a vague statement that 'the country is not getting full value in terms of human happiness for the time spent and the increasing current expenditure . . .' (p. ix). This failing is ascribed to factors such as the claimed tendency for members to concern themselves in day-to-day administration, the low calibre of officers and, more particularly, the system of committees, departments and professionals. As Dearlove notes, there remains, however, a dearth of studies which show 'just *how* these things affect council action. In effect "explanation" is made up of the slogans "committee mindedness"; "excessive departmentalism"; and professionalism' (Dearlove, 1979, p. 150).

The Royal Commission followed a very similar procedure. To a large extent '[its] analysis', Stanyer comments, 'is a highly conventional one and is not particularly derived from the evidence of witnesses or of the specially commissioned research' (Stanyer, 1973, p. 119).

The commission's handling of the crucial question of size offers the most obvious example of its determination to maintain its orthodox views as to what was wrong, however inconvenient the evidence.

The commission had available to it six separate studies of the effects of size on performance provided by its own research staff, outside bodies and two government departments (Redcliffe-Maud, 1969, para. 217):

> The over-riding impression which emerges from the three studies by outside bodies and from our own study of staffing is that size cannot statistically be proved to have a very important effect on performance. There were a few scattered instances where economies of scale seemed to be operating . . . But, in general, size did not seem to have a greater bearing on performance than some environmental characteristics of local authorities.

This conclusion appeared to undermine the most important of the grounds for reform. As Dearlove suggests (1979, p. 71), the commission had only two options:

> They could accept the evidence of the research studies, cast the orthodox rule of reform to the wind, operate outside the framework and assumptions of the conventional wisdom, and devise some alternative formula to guide the course of their re-organising endeavours. Alternatively they could stand by the orthodoxy, in which case they would need to discredit the research studies and find some alternative base from which to legitimise their approach to re-organisation.

It chose the latter course. The studies were dismissed by pointing out that they were 'the prisoners of the existing structure. Since all the statistics used were necessarily compiled on an existing local authority basis, they could not tell us how a new pattern of authorities might perform' (Redcliffe-Maud, 1969, para. 219). It was curious that this objection to the research was not raised when it was first planned, and even more curious that the commission could subsequently turn to the two departmental studies which it had sponsored, without raising similar objections, although they too were based on current practice and presumably were 'prisoners of the existing structure'.

The departmental studies were based on the views of inspectors of education and of the children's service. They did suggest that there was a positive association between size and performance and were seized on by the commission to counter the findings of the other inquiries. Yet, as one critic has noted, the studies were 'pseudo-scientific' and were 'put forward by the least disinterested bodies in the whole discussion, two departments of a service which, well in advance of the studies, was already convinced of the superiority of large authorities!' (quoted in Dearlove, 1979, p. 72). Furthermore, the commission refused to let the Local Government Operational Research Unit undertake further research into the question of size, using a model that would have overcome the criticisms it had made of studies based on existing structures (Stanyer, 1973, p. 138).

Underlying concepts

It would appear, then, that the preconceptions of the members of these two inquiries carried more weight than the findings of their researchers or the evidence presented to them. It is therefore of some importance to try to establish what frames of reference most members seemed to be operating within. Three concepts are of particular significance in the context of our study: democracy, efficiency and organisation.

Both inquiries placed great emphasis on the importance of sustaining local democracy. This task was included in the terms of reference of the commission (p. iii) and assumed as an aim by the committee: 'Our view is that . . . democratic local self-government is an essential institution . . .' (para. 250). But what does democracy mean? The committee suggests (para. 316) that

> For the health of government, whether central or local, there is a need for criticism and an understanding of public affairs; and the election of local councils at least makes this possible. 'The real strength of local government lies in the relationship between the local authority and the local public and this means a personal relationship, a state of affairs in which the public feel that the local authority and the local public service belong to them.' (Sir H. Banwell)

Seeking evidence of the health of local democracy, the committee gathered data on voting, knowledge of local councillors and services provided by the council, attendance at council meetings, and so on. It was perturbed to find low levels of public interest and involvement (para. 324):

Despite the apparently extreme democratic forms which characterise local government in this country (e.g. the large councils, the two-tier system of local authorities, the present administration by committees and the high degree of participation in the daily affairs of the authority by members) there is, undoubtedly, ignorance of the work of local government and apathy towards it. Authorities fail to 'communicate' themselves to the public; local authorities have democratic procedures to enable them to be responsive to the public and to stimulate the public's interest but these procedures appear to be in excess of what the majority of people need or want from local government as it now exists. It is a matter of concern that there should be an indefinable gulf between local authorities and the communities which they serve . . .

Similar criteria for democracy are implied in the commission's report: levels of voting, willingness to stand for office, interest in issues. By having larger authorities which would have more power, it was thought more public involvement would be generated (paras 573–5).

While both inquiries stress the importance of public involvement in elections and evidence of active interest in the processes of local government, both clearly perceive democracy as a representative rather than a participative institution. It may at first, therefore, seem paradoxical that the lack of public interest is deplored in both reports. As we point out in Chapter 8, exponents of representative democracy are likely to believe that participation so far as the majority is concerned is participation in the choice of decision-makers. High levels of public involvement beyond elections would threaten the fragile stability of the system. But, nevertheless, a certain minimum level of participation is required to 'keep the democratic method (electoral machinery) working' (Pateman, 1970, p. 14) and it seems that it was evidence that this minimum was not being achieved that worried the inquiries. If the public showed no interest in local government then the arguments against the assumption of still greater powers by central government must be weakened.

Both reports are centrally concerned with efficiency in local government. For example, the commission concluded by asserting that the new, larger authorities it advocated would produce better services and make better use of resources (paras 570–1). This assertion is based on the belief that larger authorities will be able to integrate the work of different departments more effectively and will reap the benefits of economy of scale. The committee held that efficiency could only be obtained by a streamlined organisation in which councillors restricted their involvement to the 'big decisions' and left their officers free 'fully [to] exploit their powers of initiative and expert skill', using modern management techniques as a part of the process. Yet neither report tackles squarely the challenge of defining the meaning of efficiency. It is as though the term is taken to be universally understood and politically neutral. The assumption is that all that is involved is getting the best results at the lowest costs. But the emphasis on *technique* which this focus encourages is only meaningful if there is a consensus about ends. In practice, there is seldom agreement between the many interested parties on the fundamental issues as to what services should be provided, and in what manner. For example, if the aim of a policy is to provide a standardised service to a particular client group, regardless of any variations in local conditions or individual preferences, economies of scale may result from organisation on a larger scale. But if instead it is the policy of an authority to relate the provision of a service to different local needs and individual cases, smaller units of administration may be better equipped to deliver the service. The advocacy of large, centralised authorities and increased managerial control implies, in fact, the adoption of a particular model of local government: miniature Westminsters and Whitehalls up and down the country, with popular participation restricted to the same impotent role that it has in relation to the national government.

Assumptions about the nature of organisational structure and management processes are contained in both reports but are more readily distinguished in the work of the committee. Its proposals for the elimination of many of the councils' committees, for the integration of departments, for the appointment of a chief excutive, for an inner cabinet and a managing board and for the use of advanced management techniques of all kinds (para. 230) imply a thorough-going acceptance of the precepts of scientific and classical management theory. In these theories the compliance of staff in the organisation is taken as largely unproblematical. Good organisation is principally concerned with finding the 'one best way' of carrying out the work of the organisation. It is then for management to instruct other employees in their tasks, and for these employees to obey. Consensual assumptions about the ends of local government are matched, then, by consensual assumptions about the operation of local government organisations.

How realistic are such assumptions? It is curious to find that while both inquiries drew enthusiastically on particular work rationalisation techniques developed in modern industrial and commercial management, they both completely ignored other developments in management concerned with the human element in organisation. In the 1950s and 1960s the managements of large enterprises were becoming increasingly concerned with the problems of ensuring employee compliance and commitment. Contemporary organisation theory pointed up the importance of conflicting interests within the enterprise, and emphasised the alienating effects of many of the jobs of lower-level employees. Leading companies such as ICI and Shell were re-examining their assumptions about management and organisation and actively developing more participatory contracts with their employees in attempts to win fuller commitment from them. Yet there is no hint in the report of either inquiry that such problems might exist in local government, nor that they might be aggravated in the larger, more managerially oriented organisations advocated. Did the members of the committee and commission believe that conflict and alienation only afflict industrial and commercial enterprises, and that the public service is immune? Or did these issues simply seem irrelevent to them?

Discussion

It is difficult to escape the impression that the members of both inquiries had decided on the general nature of the changes they thought necessary before they got to work. For all the evidence that was heard and research that was commissioned, neither the committee nor the commission seemed interested in testing the bases of the current orthodoxy. The ends of local government were taken as given. Reform was principally concerned with increasing its efficiency. Efficiency depended on attracting high-calibre officers and giving them the context and scope to use their skills and abilities. There is much talk in both reports about democracy, but this is clearly defined in terms of representation and not participation. No inherent conflict was perceived between the centralising and managerial reforms proposed and this kind of democracy, for it was held that it would free most members to give more time to their constituents and would persuade central government to give more powers to local authorities which would in turn attract more interest from the electors. Issues of political and organisational conflict were largely ignored in both inquiries and seem to have had little influence on their recommendations.

The proposals of the Committee on Management were well received by the government of the day and largely endorsed by the report of the study group later set up by the Secretary of State for the Environment and the local authority associations to consider management structures in the new local authorities (Bains, 1972). The proposals of the Royal Commission, for fifty-eight new large single-tier authorities responsible for all services, were accepted in principle by the Labour government but substantially revised by the succeeding Conservative government to include a second tier. Nevertheless, the reorganisation of local government went ahead in 1974 and saw the amalgamation of many of the smaller authorities in the new district, county and metropolitan district councils.

Studies of management reorganisation since Maud and Bains have been carried out by the Institute of Local Government Studies at Birmingham (Inlogov). They suggest that while in form many of the proposals of these committees have been adopted, in practice there have been difficulties in gaining the commitment of both councillors and officers to them. The number and size of committees, for instance, has been reduced but in some cases it has been found necessary to reinflate the numbers of members per committee to give them something to do (Inlogov in Dearlove, 1979, p. 168). A chief executive has been appointed in almost every authority but only in the metropolitan authorities is he anything like the policy-maker and director. Management teams have not yet developed on the Maud model. 'Few authorities have followed the orthodox advice and created a small team because of the "social problems of resentment, suspicion, and communication" where certain officers are excluded' (Dearlove, 1979, p. 172).

Political and organisational realities, it would seem, have slowed down the pace of change. Nevertheless, there has been a movement towards corporate management and where this succeeds in overcoming resistance from the old system a new order is being established. Such systems, as Dearlove notes (p. 183), emphasise

leadership and hierarchy and concentrate power into the hands of a small group of leading councillors and officers. In the wider literature of organisational sociology, this concern to create a tight, conflict-free, centrally directed, corporate, hierarchical organisation, in which professional judgement is played down, is usually seen as the very antithesis of the organisational form most conducive to genuine innovation and responsiveness.

The reorganisation of the personal social services

The reorganisation of the personal social services in England and Wales in the early 1970s provides another example of faith that reform and progress in the social services could be achieved by increased dòses of bureaucracy and professionalism. The case for some kind of reform in the provision of welfare services at the local level was widely accepted. The highly fragmented system of services for different need groups which existed at the time had been built up piecemeal as different categories of client were detached from the originally comprehensive system of the nineteenth-century Poor Law. When the last vestiges of the Poor Law were swept away in 1948 there were separate departments or sections dealing with the deprived child, the elderly and physically handicapped, the mentally ill and subnormal, the delinquent and those with need for social work support in schools, hospitals, local authority housing and various other settings.

During the 1950s and early 1960s pressure built up to rationalise this fragmented system. Social workers themselves were among the most vociferous exponents of reform. In 1966 the Seebohm Committee was set up to consider what should be done. Reporting in 1968 the committee criticised the prevailing system of personal social services on several grounds. In particular, it pointed out that people's problems seldom fell neatly within the scope of any one particular department or section. To take a not particularly unusual example, a family with a mentally ill mother and child-rearing problems related to her illness might find itself the client, at one and the same time, of the children's department, the health department, the probation office and the education welfare section of the education authority. Such fragmentation of care posed problems both of access to those seeking help and of co-ordination for those providing it. Further, small departments were unlikely to have much muscle in the fight for resources, and were obviously finding it difficult to attract sufficient trained personnel. The overall result was work of a lower quality than the public had the right to expect.

Plans for reform

The committee considered a number of alternative plans for remedying the situation and finally came down in favour of the reorganisation of the main family welfare services – child care, the elderly and physically ill and handicapped, mental health and social work in education and hospitals – in a single social services department. (It would have liked to have included probation as well, but this department was outside its terms of reference.) The establishment of such departments would, the committee argued, significantly reduce the problems of access and co-ordination. The departments would be amongst the biggest in the local authority and could be expected to attract more resources and to recruit more trained manpower. They would be large enough to maintain their own research sections which would be capable of providing them with feedback on their performance.

In recommending how the new departments should be structured and managed, four key ingredients emerge in the committee's report, each with its accompanying set of assumptions. First there was the question of leadership. The new departments should be led by social workers with administrative skills, or administrators with professional qualifications in social work. It was apparently assumed by the committee that there would be no shortage of people with the appropriate skills and qualifications to run the new unified departments although, given the predominance of small organisations in the personal social services at the time, it is by no means clear where they were expected to emerge from.

Secondly there was the issue of size. The committee's views on the size of the new departments and the area teams within them show evidence of both bureaucratic and professional criteria. It seems to have taken it for granted that administratively small organisations of the kind that predominated at the time in the personal social services were less efficient than larger ones. Economies of scale were taken as self-evident: 'an organisation with a total budget of £100,000 should be able to do more with it than the sum of the achievements of two separate organisations, each with £50,000' (Seebohm, 1968, para. 150). The committee also assumed that the larger organisation would necessarily be better placed to assess the outcome of its own work than the smaller organisation.

Nevertheless, when it came to the question of organising field services 'professional' criteria were used in assessing the appropriate size of the areas which should be established. The committee recognised two competing factors: the internal needs of the social services teams and the needs of the local community. The former were calculated exclusively in terms of the social work members of the team. The report suggested that, given the need to cover a range of specialisms, to allow for supervision, leave, sickness, and so on, ten to twelve social workers was the minimum size for a viable area team. Given the numbers of workers in the departments at the time this meant the population covered by the team would be between 50,000 and 100,000. To build close relations with the community, another key aspect of the committee's proposals, smaller areas would be desirable. However, these were to wait until more social workers became available. The internal viability of the social work team had to come first.

The importance of involving the community more fully in the work of the personal social services is the third major ingredient in the committee's proposals. It recognised that the tasks facing the new departments could not be tackled by the paid workers on their own and it was assumed that there was a substantial potential for voluntary action in the community remaining to be tapped. In particular, the help of volunteers working directly with the new departments should be sought.

Finally, it was essential if area teams were to respond flexibly and imaginatively to the problems of their localities and to tap their potential for voluntary action that area managers should be given a wide measure of discretion in their work. It was apparently assumed that such devolution of authority would be compatible with local authority tradition and practice and there would be no objections from councillors or senior officers.

The plans applied

After considerable debate and negotiation the major part of the committee's proposals was accepted by the government of the day and embodied in the Social Services Act of 1970. The new departments (minus hospital social work which was brought in in 1974, and education welfare) were established in 1971. The Seebohm Committee was confident that its proposals would lead to a better-quality service which would also reach more people. Nine years after the implementation of its main proposals, how far has its confidence proved justified?

This is a difficult question to answer, not least because the new social services departments themselves have generally failed to produce the kind of data about their performance which would allow one to assess their achievements with any confidence. Research and evaluation have in most cases been given low priority in the departments and few substantial studies of outcome in the personal social services have been undertaken by academic institutions. However, such evidence as is available is hardly reassuring. While there have been undoubted gains from integrating previously fragmented services, and it is evident that the new departments have attracted more resources and are involved with more clients, it is by no means clear that the quality of the work undertaken has substantially improved or that they have been successful in bringing about the major increase in community involvement which Seebohm regarded as central to its proposals.

As indicated in the last chapter, in the five years following the establishment of the new departments in 1971, spending on the personal social services increased much faster than public expenditure as a whole. But it is all too easy to confuse increases in inputs with improvements in output. To show that more resources were poured into a service is not necessarily to prove that the service has improved to a corresponding extent, or even that it has improved at all. Indeed, such evidence as there is about the performance of the personal social services since reorganisation (although much of it is no more than circumstantial) would appear to illustrate this point only too well. In spite of the injection of additional resources the preventive, community-oriented approach advocated by Seebohm has eluded the personal social services. The continued reliance on a reactive bureaucratic system, tempered by a limited degree of professional autonomy for the social workers within it, gives little grounds for confidence about increasing effectiveness. The situation can be thrown into clearer relief by taking the examples of two client groups served by the departments: the elderly, and families and children.

The elderly. The declared policy of the personal social services towards the elderly is to enable them to stay in the community in their own homes, as long as possible, wherever it is their wish to do so. The prerequisites for this, as physical capacity declines, is practical help with domestic and personal tasks, and such social interaction as the old person may need to maintain his or her morale. Most of the frail elderly receive such support from their own networks of family, friends and neighbours (and in the case of the better off, through paid help). But two groups in particular are at risk: first, those whose informal networks are in danger of breaking down as the support tasks become more onerous, and secondly, those with little or no informal support at all. It is in work with these two groups that the social services department might be expected to make its greatest contribution to the prevention or delay of admission to residential care. However, to undertake such work effectively the SSD needs not only adequate substitute resources such as home helps, meals on wheels, and so on, but also early knowledge of those at risk, and good information about such caring networks as they possess.

Available evidence indicates that most SSDs have neither the organisational structures nor sufficient staff interest and commitment to acquire and use such information. Most area teams remain large and cover populations of 50,000 and upwards. Most do not assign their workers to local neighbourhoods or 'patches' within these areas and in consequence are insufficiently soaked in knowledge of their communities to get advance warning about those old people who may shortly be in need of help, or those caring networks that are feeling the strain and will need support if they are not to collapse. Of course, substantial numbers of the elderly at risk are known to area teams (Goldberg and Warburton, 1979), but what proportion these form of those most in need of help can only be guessed, and all too often referral is only made when a case has reached crisis point and it may be too late for preventive support. The problem of the frail elderly is compounded by the tendency for most social workers to dislike working with them (Parsloe and Stevenson, 1978; Rees, 1978; Goldberg and Warburton, 1979) and the pressures from the media, politicians and the 'public' to give priority to other client groups, especially children. Where the elderly are concerned 'community care' may all too often be a euphemism for community neglect (Opit, 1977).

Families and children. The responsibilities of the new departments for deprived children and children at risk of mental or physical cruelty have probably attracted more attention than any other aspects of their work. In particular, cases of non-accidental injury to children known to the authority, as in the Maria Colwell and Stephen Meurs cases, have emphasised the importance attached to the protective or supervisory role of the SSDs. However, most people would probably accept that the duties of the departments should be defined more broadly in terms of preventive work *before* care or supervision orders become necessary. To operate a strategy of this kind would seem to require (1) early knowledge of those at risk in the community, (2) good co-operation with other agencies involved, (3) social work skills to support the families concerned and to bring about changes in behaviour which will enable at least the large majority to resume full responsibility for care of their children.

There is little evidence to suggest that most SSDs have created the structures in which the first two of these conditions can be satisfied, nor that training and practice has created on a widespread basis the social work skills referred to in the third. As in the case of the elderly, in most departments the service remains centralised. Workers are not deployed in such a way as to have intimate links with the community of the kind required for good information and easy access. The Maria Colwell inquiry illustrated both the difficulty of knowing what was going on in a particular community and the barriers to access to the departments by lay people wanting to give information (*Committee of Inquiry ... Maria Colwell*, 1974, paras 200, 206, 207).

In spite of the integration of some local authority social services in the new departments, a wide range of other agencies still exists, including health, housing, education and police, which are likely to have dealings with families at risk. Formal interchange of information between bureaucracies is notoriously slow and uncertain, not only because the procedures involved may be cumbersome but also because perceptions and priorities in the bodies concerned may differ (*Committee of Inquiry ... Maria Colwell*, 1974, paras 183, 193). While area teams still cover large populations, social workers are likely to have to liaise with a bewildering variety and number of other agencies. Small wonder area managers often complain that it takes a new worker at least a year to get to know his or her area and that it is often difficult for individual workers to build up good relationships with other agencies.

Even when families and children in need of help have been identified, there remains considerable doubt about the capacity of social work to help solve their problems. The casework approach, which is usually used with such clients, remains on trial. Such evaluative studies as exist have come up with negative or at best inconclusive results.

The recent National Institute for Social Work study of a SSD found that while the team involved devoted most of its casework activity to family and children work, the clients involved were the most dissatisfied of the people helped by the department, and progress was rated lower by staff than with any other category of clients. The researchers expressed their own disquiet at the manner in which family cases had come to dominate the departments (Goldberg and Warburton, 1979, p. 129):

> We have been impressed . . . by the amount of social work time (as well as other resources such as day and residential care) taken up by a comparatively small number of chronically disorganised and disturbed families. The families appear to be in an almost constant state of crisis.

The most highly trained and experienced members of the social work team were allocated to this work at the expense of other client groups. This was partly as an insurance policy against the recurrence of Maria Colwell type cases. It was also doubtless affected by social workers' well-established preference for working with this client group. But even given current doubts about the effectiveness of casework, many social workers remain curiously conservative in their practice. The advantages of short-term over long-term methods of intervention, for example, and the potential of auxiliary help, although now well established, appear to have made little impact on practice (Holme and Maizels, 1978; Parsloe and Stevenson, 1978; Goldberg and Warburton, 1979).

Discussion

The Seebohm Committee's vision of the future envisaged a system in which the best advantages of bureaucracy, professionalism and community involvement would be combined. It was an attractive vision to many who read the report, but the departments which have been set up since 1971 bear little resemblance to it. All too often they appear much like other local authority bureaucracies, hierarchical, rule-bound, slow to respond to change. Typically, professionalism is synonomous with an orientation to casework, and community involvement, far from being a central feature of the departmental strategy, is a fringe activity relegated to low-status 'community workers'. The stance of the SSD is more correctly characterised as reactive then preventive.

What went wrong? The planned reorganisation was more

imaginative than many proposals emanating from government committees of inquiry. The need for more flexible, decentralised forms of organisation was clearly recognised. Yet the committee seems to have given curiously little thought to the practicalities of its proposals, in particular underestimating the rigidity of both bureaucratic and professional ideologies and practice, and the difficulties of recruiting managers with the skills their scheme required.

Most important of all, however, was the failure of the committee to work out the implications of a preventive strategy for the level at which services should be organised. Instead of starting from the requirements of a preventive strategy and then considering the deployment of resources, the committee took as given the need to have teams of social workers not smaller than a given number. This ruled out the possibility of much smaller areas of administration in which other workers such as home helps or social work assistants might have been given more prominent roles, and in which much closer relations with the community might have been built up.

The new bureaucracy was seen by the committee as bringing economies of scale, better co-ordination, more resources. But it was to be tempered by a highly decentralised system of area teams. It was never suggested that such devolution of power might be incompatible with the traditions of local government administration. The creation of the social services committee involved the setting up of a powerful new department. Given the representative system of government, it is the task of the committee to control the department. The bureaucracy is the servant of the authority and as such must be answerable to it. If a substantial degree of authority were to be given to area managers, what would the role of councillors be then? How can devolution be made compatible with accountability? A few authorities (such as Stockport) have tried to find solutions by experimenting with area management of a whole range of services. But this is not the norm and one might have expected the committee in making proposals which flew in the face of traditional practice to indicate ways in which they could be made acceptable.

A further curious gap in the committee's thinking concerned the supply of managers for the SSDs. Great stress was laid on the need for administrative skills both at director level and at area level. But all line management posts must be filled by qualified social workers. Where was a sufficient supply of social workers with administrative skill to come from? Before reorganisation most of the specialist departments were small and their management called for only rudimentary administrative skills. The large SSDs that replaced them were quite another matter. The skills needed at the top were at least of an order comparable to those of managing director of a medium-to large-sized firm, and at area level the call for a high measure of autonomy, creativity and flexibility implied skills of the kind described by Burns and Stalker (1966) in their account of 'organic' management in the electronics industry. How could hundreds of such managers be found overnight when the proposed Act came into force? Most social workers are attracted to their profession by the prospect of one-to-one work, not social administration. There was no reason to think that there were large untapped reservoirs of managerial ability in their ranks, let alone people with the special qualities required by organic management.

The committee gave remarkably little thought to the whole question of professional ideologies in social work, and their compatibility with the new organisation it was proposing. While the issue of generic versus specialist caseloads was explored, the broader issue of who should decide priorities between different categories of clients – social workers or the community – was not. The committee did recognise the need for closer relationships between training institutions and the departments if training was to be more realistic, but it did not define in what ways this should change the end product of training. In the event, most courses still seem to concentrate on casework skills as the core of social work training. While most institutions also introduce notions of community work and of organisation and management, in the large majority they would appear to have peripheral rather than core status. They do not define the student's main expectations of the job he is preparing for. Most new social workers still appear to cling to the notion that *real* social work is intensive casework and that any other activities are somehow inferior and marginal.

This short case study of reorganisation in the personal social services has necessarily emphasised the role of the Seebohm Committee. It would be a mistake to imply, however, that somehow it bears all the responsibility for the changes which followed. In so far as its proposals were largely accepted not only by the professionals but also by both political parties, it seems clear that its arguments had wide appeal, and its proposals conform to current notions of rationalisation and reform. The more radical proposals of the committee for community involvement and preventive work may have been regarded by many as mere rhetoric. The important changes involved the creation of tidy bureaucracies with properly trained and resourced staff. That was progress enough.

Health service reorganisation

The third and perhaps the most ill-starred major reorganisation was that of the health service. In 1974 the tripartite organisation created when the NHS was set up in 1948, consisting of hospitals, local authority health services and family practitioner services, was scrapped. In its place was erected a national pyramid of heroic proportions in which all the separate services were unified. At the base were district management teams, over them area health authorities, and at the pinnacle the secretary of state. The reorganisation was a massive and costly operation which has already come in for devastating criticism, even from many of those who were originally its most enthusiastic exponents. The stages in the process leading up to the reform furnish further evidence on the ways in which those in government and the civil service perceived the main purposes of a social service, their assumptions about the nature of good administration and their views on the role of the public both in the procedures of reform and in the management of the resulting organisation.

We consider first why reorganisation was considered necessary, secondly how the reforms were devised, and finally how they were applied and with what results.

The case for reform

The main impetus for reform came from within the health service itself, and to a lesser extent from politicians. There is little to suggest that any significant pressure for change came from users of the service at large. Indeed, such surveys of public opinion of the health service as were carried out in the 1960s 'tended to show the NHS as a highly used and much appreciated service' (Draper *et al.*, 1976, p. 259).

Two kinds of factors contributed to the arguments for reform: the substantive criticisms of the organisation and management of the service and precipitating conditions of the late 1960s and early

1970s. Perhaps the most important of the substantive issues was the growing size and cost of the NHS.

Evidence also began to accumulate of a number of imbalances in the service. In particular attention was focused on the wide variations in provision in different parts of the country, the per capita expenditure for patients varying as much as 100 per cent between regions. Imbalances of another type related to the different categories of illness. It became clear that hospitals dealing with acute conditions were far better funded and staffed than those dealing with the long-term sick and mentally ill. The tripartite division of functions itself was the subject of sharp criticism for the split it had created between general practice and the hospital, and between hospital and the community services of the local authority.

The process of reform began long before the 1974 reorganisation and, indeed, can be regarded in itself as an important influence in the build-up of pressure for more thoroughgoing change. The Ministry of Health gradually began to take a more directive role in the running of the service and *laissez-faire* policies of the early days were replaced 'by the language of priorities and value for money' (Brown, 1979, p. 13). The ministry strengthened its information-gathering and began to encourage more systematic planning in the regions. In 1962 it published a ten-year plan for the development of the hospital service. Revelations of mismanagement in hospitals for long-stay patients led to the establishment of minimum standards for such institutions and the introduction of an inspectorate. Reforms were instituted in the nursing service and in the role of doctors in hospital management. The emphasis on increased rationalisation and central control, then, was already clearly visible before the publication of the first Green Paper on NHS reorganisation in 1968.

Two more immediate factors seem to have been important in precipitating change. The first was the impetus to reform created by the establishment of inquiries in two other fields, the Royal Commission on Local Government and the Seebohm Committee on the personal social services. Both, as we have seen, recommended major reorganisation. Stirring changes were afoot. People were thinking of reform on a grand scale. If important changes were needed in the health service, something beyond the scope of the piecemeal improvements that had been gradually introduced over the years, this was surely the time to make them. In particular, since local government was involved, it made good sense to aim to inaugurate the reforms at the same time. As soon as 1 April 1974 had been fixed as the starting date for the new local authorities, this too became the target for the NHS reformers and a respectable reason to make haste had been created.

A second precipitating factor is inherent in the parliamentary system itself. Given the limited five-year term of a government and allowing for the period required for consultation, drafting, debate and planning for implementation, politicians have every motive for encouraging expedition in the handling of important reforms of this nature for fear than an electoral upset will bring all their plans to dust. Labour lost its proposed reform of the NHS by starting the process too late in its term. The Conservative government returned in 1970 was clearly determined not to be caught out in the same way.

The arena for debate

The manner in which a government opens its proposals for important legislation to public debate reveals much about its views on the proper processes of decision-making in a democracy as well as indicating its belief about which particular groups really matter if it is to get its way. It might have been expected that changes on the scale that were being considered for the NHS in the late 1960s would have justified the careful consideration of a committee of inquiry or a Royal Commission. However, it appears that both the Labour government of the day and the Conservative administration which succeeded it in 1970 were sufficiently convinced that they knew what kind of reform was needed to dispense with such elaborate and time-consuming procedures. The main aim of both parties, in turn, seems to have been to assure themselves of the support of the principal interest groups in the NHS itself, and more especially of the doctors.

The Labour government issued its first consultative document, proposing a unified service, in 1968. Criticisms, especially from the medical profession, led to a second Green Paper in 1970. In theory, the publication of a consultative document offers the electorate as a whole the chance to discuss the issues involved. In practice, given the remoteness which most citizens in a parliamentary system feel from government, public debate is unlikely unless it is deliberately stimulated by those in power at the time or by the media. No such encouragement was given on the appearance of either Green Paper. Proposals from the incoming Conservative government were given an even more restricted airing. The secretary of state's consultative document of 1971 was not made generally available but was sent only to 'interested parties'. Furthermore, with the excuse of the 1974 deadline only two months was allowed for comments and opinions. There was no invitation to the public to share in the debate before the government's proposals were formed up into a White Paper the following year. Meanwhile detailed planning for the proposed changes was already under way in the DHSS two years before the reorganisation Bill became law. The media did little or nothing to try to remedy this deliberate by-passing of public debate. Peter Draper and his colleagues in the Department of Community Medicine at Guy's Hospital monitored press, television and radio coverage of the reforms. They noted that the first BBC television broadcast on the reorganisation was not until after the Bill had received royal assent, that press coverage was almost as late, and that such as there was tended to concentrate on a minor clause of the Bill relating to family planning. He and his colleagues came into frequent contact with producers and journalists during this time and were appalled at their ignorance of the issues. 'It does not seem too harsh a judgement – indeed it was often their own – that with very few exceptions, broadcasting staff were largely ignorant of even the essential features of the re-organisation a year after the "consultative document" had appeared . . .' (Draper *et al.*, 1976, p. 271).

Directions for reform

In theory, those considering reform in the organisation of the NHS in the late 1960s and early 1970s could have explored a whole range of alternatives to the present structure. Unification under centralised control was by no means the only feasible solution for the problems that had been identified. For example, the integration of services at local level did not necessarily require the construction of an elaborate national framework to control it. An alternative would have been to increase the autonomy of local teams, build in staff and public participation and encourage the development of flexible, organic management systems, capable of co-ordinating with related services in the local authority, and responding to change in ways that suited local circumstances. A few voices were in fact raised in favour of this kind of development (Draper and Smart, 1972) but they received scant attention from either major political party.

In their turn both Labour and Conservative governments had made it clear that they favoured a unified and centralised health service. Their broad aims 'appear almost identically in the two

Green Papers and in the 1972 White Paper, differences being either in political rhetoric or details of implementation' (Brown, 1979, p. 38). The most significant discrepancy between the two governments' plans was over public participation. Labour's scheme, which had only been developed in outline, made provision for public involvement in the supervision of services at the local level. The Conservatives replaced this by a purely consultative role, creating community health councils for the purpose.

The Conservative plan, which was embodied in the 1973 Act, was to establish a hierarchy of three tiers under the DHSS: the regional health authorities, of which there were to be fourteen in England, under them about ninety area health authorities, responsible for some two hundred district management teams. Political participation in these bodies was to be kept to a minimum. The RHAs were to be appointed by the secretary of state, a majority of members of the AHAs would be chosen by the RHAs and the DMTs would be managed entirely by professionals and administrators. The thrust of the new organisation was unapologetically managerial. As Sir Keith Joseph said of the proposal in his introduction to the consultative document, 'their essence – and their basic difference from earlier proposals – is the emphasis they place on effective management'.

Working out the management arrangements

The development of a uniform national structure to run the health services implied at least a degree of corresponding uniformity in management, organisation and practice. However, the ways in which this could be worked out were not given. For example, there could have been a thorough programme of consultation throughout the existing service. But the methods in fact chosen to devise the management arrangements were worked out largely in the abstract in the apparent belief that the necessary knowledge and expertise was already available and that the new order once designed could be imposed from the centre. A study group, consisting mainly of civil servants and health service administrators, was appointed to handle the matter. The group was advised by two teams of consultants, one from the American firm of McKinsey and the other from Brunel University. Both teams appeared to make a considerable impact, to judge from the character of the final document produced by the study group in 1972, *Management Arrangements for the Reorganised National Health Service*, known as the Greybook.

In the view of a recent student of the reorganised NHS, R. G. S. Brown, the Brunel advisors seem to have been particularly influential. At the time the unit concerned, the Health Services Organisation Unit, practised a technique called 'social analysis' which entailed the classification of role structures in an organisation by elaborate discussions with those holding the positions concerned. Some of the key concepts developed in the Greybook and later applied in the reorganised NHS originate from this approach, including the notions of consensus management and the monitoring relationships between one level of officials and another. The fuzziness of the administrators' role is also partly attributable to these ideas, since although social analysis aimed at scientific clarity it yielded a most incomplete view of the functioning of organisations. The naivety of the Brunel approach is implied by the enthusiasm with which it was adopted by professional interest groups 'anxious to thwart an accountability system which might threaten their own autonomy' (Brown, 1979, p. 47).

Be this as it may, when the Greybook was published in 1972 it contained probably the most detailed and comprehensive account of roles, responsibilities and procedures that has ever been produced for a government bureaucracy in advance of its creation. Although it was emphasised at the time that the document was not intended as the last word on the subject, and that it could be criticised and modified, relatively few changes were introduced before 1974. It is hardly surprising if, given the pace and complexity of change, it came to acquire the status of a rulebook or blueprint by those preparing to implement the new organisation.

The new organisation in action

How closely did the new health service resemble the efficient, streamlined, centralised organisation planned by Sir Keith Joseph and his team? In form at least the new model was highly centralised, with the DHSS controlling the planning cycle and the distribution of resources. Authority was delegated, not decentralised or devolved. Political involvement was kept to a minimum by the central control of appointments at region and area. The favourite press epithet for the community health councils was 'toothless watchdogs', since even when strengthened subsequently by Barbara Castle they could bark but not bite. Health needs were defined on technocratic not political grounds.

But if these were believed to be the necessary preconditions for effective management of the service, something was badly wrong in the planners' calculations. There is a growing consensus that the introduction of the remodelled service was highly disruptive of ongoing administration of the NHS and financially very costly, and that once established the new system has shown alarming signs of galloping bureaucratic arteriosclerosis which can only be cured by yet more reorganisational surgery.

Brown's detailed study of the process of reorganisation of the NHS in Humberside enabled him to pick out some of the main costs of the changeover. First, it was highly disruptive of ongoing work. Secondly, it was difficult to hold operating costs down during the upheaval of change, and more or less impossible to recover lost ground once the changes were completed. Thirdly, it was expensive in manpower. Many good staff took the opportunity offered of early retirement and were lost to the service. Various categories of employees were able to use negotiations over their roles in the new service to increase their pay substantially. The emphasis on keeping to a tight timetable meant that people became more concerned with maintaining the momentum of change than with its underlying purposes. Perhaps his most salutary conclusion concerns the over-optimistic views of the reformers and the need for careful piloting of new organisational forms before wholesale commitment to them (Brown, 1979, pp. 199–200).

Several of Brown's criticisms are echoed in the *Report of the Royal Commission on the National Health Service* (Merrison, 1979); but the report goes on to find still more fundamental faults in the heart of the new organisation itself. It finds control over-centralised, too many levels of management, the system of professional consultation too elaborate and organisational forms too rigid.

The commission was obviously amazed at the extent to which the bureaucrats had had their way and a uniform system of management had been imposed throughout the country (para. 20.9):

It seems to us obvious enough that the way health care should be brought to the people of Wester Ross and to the people of Tower Hamlets will be entirely different; and that there is no reason, other than the false god of administrative tidiness, why the service management arrangements should be the same or, indeed, why they should even resemble each other to any great degree.

It is the impression of the commission that management

arrangements have 'tended to be inflexible and to follow too closely the guidance issued by the health departments' (para. 20.10).

NHS workers have complained without cease that management decisions are removed from the people best suited to make them. Despite the emphasis in the 1971 Consultative Document and the 1972 White Paper on 'maximum delegation downwards matched by accountability upwards' it is all too clear that the emphasis has been on the latter (para. 20.11).

The commission goes on to criticise the declining quality of hospital management, poor financial management, and many other aspects of the new model. Although the commissioners are too polite to say so in as many words, only five years after its inception the reorganised health service has been found defective in the very areas in which it was supposed to be strongest – those of efficient and effective management.

Conclusions

It would seem clear from these examples that the more important assumptions which we identified in earlier phases of collectivism and centralisation (Chapters 2 and 3) were still alive and well in government circles in the 1960s and early 1970s. These assumptions, without doing too much violence to the variations described in the case studies, can now be summarised under the following seven heads:

(1) *The feasibility and desirability of the standard solution.* It is both possible and desirable to find standard packages for application throughout the country. More room was left by the Seebohm proposals for individual initiative in the planning of local social services, but even here local authorities were not left the right to choose whether or not they should have an integrated department.

(2) *Major changes in the organisation of a service should be planned and introduced by central government.* This is the logical corollary of (1).

(3) *Larger organisations are likely to be more efficient than small organisations.* A number of reasons are advanced for this belief: (*a*) it is held that economies of scale can be obtained in

larger organisations through such advantages as specialisation of staff and functions, and the elimination of duplication of facilities; (*b*) it is also argued that staff of higher calibre can be attracted to larger organisations; (*c*) the integration of fragmented but related activities is facilitated by construction of larger organisations.

(4) *Management of public services will be most efficient if designed on scientific, rational principles.* These principles, and the modern techniques based on them, will ensure the most efficient use of public resources. The compliance of staff can be taken for granted and consequently there is no need to adapt managerial systems to embody notions of either the neo-human relations or the conflict schools, as some industrial concerns have done.

(5) *Users' role in the management of social services and local government should be marginal.* While the user has rights to express his/her views about the kinds of service he/she wants, the proper means for channelling such views is the representative system. A case for more direct consultation may exist in some cases (although the logic for it is not clear), as in the example of the CHCs, but this is not to concede the right to any direct involvement in management, since management and representation are separate, mutually disruptive functions.

(6) *Efficiency is more important than democracy.* In almost all democratic organisations there are likely to be conflicts between the view that major decisions should be governed by technical or managerial criteria alone and the view that they should also be submitted to democratic processes. In the reorganisations of local government and the NHS when the choice had to be made between efficiency and democracy it was always democracy that was sacrificed.

(7) *Major changes in organisation can be successfully designed and introduced without prior testing on a smaller scale.* Although the advantages of piloting changes in organisation may be recognised, it tends to be considered politically unrealistic to propose this method of developing new structures and practices, and perfectly feasible to get by without it.

These assumptions, then, represent a mixture of value judgements about the way in which services *ought* to be run and hypotheses about what makes for efficient services. But the two are inextricably linked. The value judgements concern the desirability of standard organisational solutions to social problems and the exclusion of the citizen from direct involvement in the management of services. As we shall show in Chapters 8–11, however, both matters may affect the quality and quantity of statutory services. Variations in local conditions may call for variations in the organisational responses. Direct citizen participation in the provision of services may be an essential part of strategies to increase the responsiveness of services and augment the resources available to them.

As to the hypotheses about the factors which make for efficient organisation, these remain either untested or tested and found wanting. The case studies have shown that there is no convincing evidence that larger organisations are necessarily more cost-effective than smaller ones, or that they can attract people of higher calibre. Empirical studies of local government and social services institutions show that they are in no way immune from the problems of compliance and conflict which are everyday concerns in commercial enterprises. It may for one reason or another be difficult for higher civil servants and others involved in planning management systems to acknowledge the existence of such problems, but this does not make them go away. The evidence of the consequences of changes introduced in each of the three areas considered in the case studies shows the high cost of moving directly from grand design to implementation without any serious attempt to pilot the changes.

In sum, the assumptions on which major changes have been made in social services and local government institutions have more the character of a mythology than a set of principles founded on well-tested experience. In particular, the mythology is one which serves to insulate managers and professionals from the demands and criticisms of consumers and lower-ranking employees by arguing that the representation of interests is something that should be carried on through separate political institutions.

CHAPTER 6

The Other Three Sectors

The main weight of our discussion has been directed at the statutory services, since they are the instruments of public policy. But they are far from being the only providers of care and services. Indeed it is one of our main criticisms of them that too often they behave as if they were. This chapter therefore looks at the three other sources of care and services – the informal, the voluntary and the commercial sectors – and seeks to outline their present roles and what determines the nature of those roles. In Chapters 9 and 10 we look at ways in which they might come to play a greater role.

The informal sector

Most of the care that is provided for dependent people living in their own homes comes not from the state, nor from voluntary organisations, nor from commercial sources, but from family, friends and neighbours. Such everyday unofficial help has come to be referred to as the informal system of care. Given its widely acknowledged importance there is remarkably little systematic evidence on the character of this system as a whole. Consequently our picture of it has to be constructed from mainly piecemeal evidence, first on the nature of informal institutions in general, secondly on the support provided for specific groups such as the elderly and handicapped.

The core of the informal sector remains the family. Studies of the family have become increasingly rare in recent years as sociological fashion has swung away from empirical analysis of the social structure. However, work carried out in the 1950s and early 1960s indicated that, in spite of the widely held view that the extended family was rapidly disintegrating under the pressures of industrial society, in a modified form it was alive and well (Shanas *et al.*, 1968; Moroney, 1976). It was clear that kinship bonds typically reached well beyond the nuclear family of husband, wife and their children. The wider family was confirmed in these studies to be a source of identity and affect, as well as the basis for the exchange of practical help.

There are few studies of neighbourhood and friendship patterns in this country which shed light on informal caring relationships in contexts outside the family. Work in the United States has suggested the importance of recognising different types of neighbourhood according to the degree of identification with an area, social exchange between neighbours and linkage with the wider community. Using criteria of these kinds a continuum of different neighbourhood types can be distinguished, from 'integral', at one extreme, to 'anomic' at the other, and variations in the use of formally organised social services are shown to be related to position on the continuum (D. I. Warren, 1978). Another significant theme in American research has been the study of key individuals in neighbourhoods who act as unofficial advisers. Their help is often sought well beyond their own circle of family and friends. Such people are sometimes referred to as 'gate-keepers' since they often act as referring agents to a range of sources of help, informal, voluntary and statutory. In the United States such natural helpers have been found in every walk of life from barbers and bartenders to lollipop ladies and local chemists (Collins and Pancoast, 1976).

While neither of these perspectives on local neighbourhood networks has yet been developed in this country, given the many similarities between our societies there is no reason to believe that when research is undertaken it will not uncover broadly similar features. In the meantime, the nearest relevant work has been concerned with neighbouring, rather than neighbourhoods, and has taken as its focus the many good neighbour schemes organised up and down the country. This has thrown some light on the place of neighbourly help as opposed to other kinds of informal care (Abrams, 1980, p. 15):

> The bulk of helping reported as 'neighbourhood care' turns out to be kin care . . . Beyond that, our strongest bases of informal social care are those of the non-located moral communities associated with churches, races, friendship groups and certain occupational groups – not neighbourhoods. Neighbours and local communities come a very poor third.

Studies of client groups

The over-riding importance of the family in the provision of informal care and the significance of this contribution in the total pattern of care to dependent people living in the community is amply and consistently demonstrated in the various client group studies carried out in Britain over the last two decades. To take the largest single dependent category, the infirm elderly, Shanas and her colleagues have shown how the large majority of this group rely almost entirely on their families and to a lesser extent on their friends and neighbours for help with their housework, in preparing meals, in shopping, in bathing themselves, and for help when they are bedfast. Only in a small minority of cases did the community care services of the social services department carry the main burden of caring. For instance, in the care of the bedfast elderly, family, friends and neighbours provided help with housework in 85 per cent of the cases (80 per cent family, 5 per cent friends and neighbours), compared with 15 per cent by the social services. Where shopping was involved the figures were 88 per cent family, 6 per cent friends and neighbours, 6 per cent social services. In the provision of meals informal care was equally important with the family providing 88 per cent, friends and neighbours 6 per cent, compared with 7 per cent from the social services (Shanas *et al.*, 1968, p. 122; figures rounded).

Taking the same client group, it has been shown that family structure is closely related to the risk of admission to an old people's home. Old people with families are far less likely to be admitted to institutions than those without, and those with very small families are more likely to be admitted than those with larger families (Townsend, 1965).

Studies of other client groups living in the community tell much the same story. The mentally handicapped, the physically handicapped, the long-term sick have all been shown to rely heavily on informal support, mainly drawn from the family (Hewitt, 1972; Bayley, 1973; Sainsbury, 1974). Informal advice and care has also been shown to be of major importance in family crises of a more acute character such as terminal illness (Cartwright *et al.*, 1973) and coronary heart disease (Finlayson and McEwen, 1977, ch. 12).

To acknowledge the central role of the informal sector in providing community care is not to imply its contribution is low cost, nor that it is invulnerable. The studies of individual client groups make it clear that the work of caring often falls largely on one person, usually a close relative, typically a woman, and can dominate her life. Much of the tending involved may be physically and emotionally demanding and the extent to which the burden can be rendered tolerable in such cases is likely to turn on the degree of back-up support the helpers receive. Where informal networks are restricted or weak this may well depend on the local social services department.

Factors affecting the extent and quality of informal care

Although we are short on knowledge of the contemporary family and neighbourhoods as social institutions, the evidence briefly outlined above on the care of particular client groups in the community provides some pointers as to the factors which are likely to affect the extent and quality of informal care. Three major factors have been identified: the extent and strength of family networks; the linkage of individuals in this network to other 'moral' communities; and the character of the neighbourhood in which the individual lives. But important as the informal sector now is, there are a number of trends which suggest that in the future it could become less important, or at any rate that its form may be modified.

These trends relate both to the availability of carers and to the numbers needing care. A factor likely to diminish the availability of carers is the entry of married women into the labour force. In 1951 22 per cent of them were in paid employment and in 1971 42 per cent, while the figure projected for 1991 is 56 per cent (*Social Trends*, 1979). Another factor is declining family and household size. Whereas those now in their eighties usually have a large number of surviving siblings, children, grandchildren, nephews and nieces, the generation which will reach pensionable age in the 1990s will have relatively far fewer. David Eversley (Eversley, forthcoming) has made an interesting calculation which shows that the typical couple married in 1920 and still alive today has forty-two living female relatives, of whom fourteen are not working. In contrast the typical couple married in 1950 are likely, when they reach 80, to have only eleven living female relatives, of whom only three will not be in paid jobs. A further consideration is the likelihood that due to geographical mobility fewer of these surviving relatives will live near enough to help.

Increasing needs for care are likely to arise from the number of people aged over 75, which is projected to rise by one-third of a million in the 1980s. The growing instability of the family also has major implications. Thus the number of one-parent families seems to have gone up by a third between 1971 and 1976 (Leete, 1978) and promises to go on rising.

However, it would be premature to assume that all these trends inevitably and necessarily point towards a decline in the relative importance of informal care. Thus divorce and remarriage mean that growing numbers of children will have two parents plus two step-parents, so re-creating in a new form the more extensive kinship networks of earlier generations. The effect this is likely to have on the availability of care for children and for future generations of the elderly will depend in part on the norms that develop around these step-relationships. It is also possible to envisage a growing caring role for households not centred on a nuclear family. Thus the situation is a fluid one which could be influenced by official policies. In discussing these policies it is helpful to distinguish between those of central and those of local government.

Central government

In a very real sense the provision of almost all informal care in the community relies to some degree on the support of the social security system. Benefits such as those for the retired, the disabled and the chronically sick, and for those who give up their jobs to care for the dependent, are often a precondition of care in the community. It is far from clear, however, to what extent an understanding of the factors affecting such care has influenced policy-making in this field. It can be argued that the prevailing levels of basic support for those who need care and the special allowances for those who stay at home to provide it fail to recognise the real costs involved and are quite inadequate. Only those who can supplement state support from their own private means can hope to get by without great hardship.

Secondly, as one of us has pointed out elsewhere (Hadley, 1976), a whole range of statutory policies not directly concerned with social care may intimately affect the strength and even the very existence of informal caring networks.

Our knowledge of just how such networks are born and develop is still minimal but it is obvious enough that kinship and neighbourhood relationships will become most firmly established where there is a measure of stability in the population. It follows, therefore, that plans concerning re-development and re-housing, changes in local employment opportunities, growth or reduction of local transport systems, all of which can deeply affect the stability of an area, are of the first importance in a policy aimed to strengthen informal care. More specifically, the policies of local employers are likely to be of considerable importance since at a time when it is becoming increasingly common for both husband and wife to work, the very possibility of providing care at home may depend on having flexible working hours. Government example, and pressure on other employers, could be a key factor in achieving this. At present, however, there is little evidence to suggest that most policy makers in any of these fields pay a great deal of attention to such questions. Where strong community networks emerge and survive these developments seldom owe much to government planning.

Local government services and local health services

The supply of services to the dependent person living in the community and to those supporting him or her can make a vital difference to the capacity of the system of informal care to cope. The support of the home help, warden, social worker, occupational therapist, community nurse, doctor and others, and the advice and practical services they can offer, such as laundry, meals, aids and adaptations, day care and short stay in residential homes, can make the difference between a tolerable and intolerable existence for both carer and cared for. Already a significant proportion of local authority and health service budgets is devoted to the provision of such resources. Yet there are grounds for concern, partly because the total input appears to be too low, partly because the best use is not being made of such resources as are currently available. For example, one study of the elderly sick living at home judged that about one-third were receiving inadequate care (Opit, 1977) and another showed that in many cases the precipitating causes leading to the admission of the elderly to a geriatric hospital were associated with inadequate medical advice and treatment, and insufficient back-up from social services (Sanford, 1975).

Another area in which the use of existing resources appears inadequate is the organisation of area social services teams. There is some evidence that these teams are not deployed in the best way to obtain good information about informal caring systems and their needs. In consequence, they are poorly placed to judge how to make the best use of their resources in support of these systems and all too often only learn about people in need of help when their problems have reached crisis proportions and the difficulties and costs of intervening are multiplied (Hadley, 1981).

A somewhat similar point may be made about the relationships between local community health services and informal care. Although the GP is likely to seem much more accessible than the area social services team his interpretation of his duties is all too often a defensive one – waiting for the patient to make his problems known – rather than a preventive one.

In sum, both nationally and locally the policies of the statutory social services towards the informal sector appear to be haphazard, piecemeal and half-hearted. It seems there is a long road to travel from the tangible certainties of the bricks and mortar of the old people's home and the hospital to the less visible but often more effective services provided in the community.

The voluntary sector

Whereas the informal sector consists of activities that are not part of any organisation, the voluntary sector is made up of organisations. However, like the informal sector, most of the work of the voluntary sector finds no place in statistics about the social services or in computations of GNP, since it is not represented in cash transactions. But this is not true of the whole of the voluntary sector since it spans a great diversity of activities and forms, ranging from organisations no less formal than those found in the statutory sector to some that are so informal that they hardly merit the term organisation. This diversity, and the lack of systematic data, make the voluntary sector difficult to generalise about. However, research arising from the Wolfenden Committee on Voluntary Organisations (Wolfenden, 1977; Hatch 1980a) does now provide at least a sketch map of the sector.

Perhaps its most formal element is the established national agencies, many of which started off as the initiators of new services before the creation of the welfare state, and now provide a professional service with paid staff. In some ways they are not fundamentally different from the bureaucratically organised, professional services delivered by social services departments. However, they are often much more specialised in the needs they seek to meet and the skills they deploy. Beyond this they add an element of diversity and choice and sources of innovation. They do also provide additional resources, though the current tendency is for organisations like Barnado's, the Royal National Institute for the Blind and the NSPCC to become more dependent on statutory funding, usually in the form of fees for services.

There are, too, numerous smaller, more recently established voluntary organisations whose work is also mainly carried out by paid staff, but which tend to depend on grants from central and local government, often provided through the Urban Programme. Their existence is evidence of the recognition by government that, particularly in inner city areas, direct statutory provision is not always the best way of responding to social problems. Hence the variety of grant-aided community projects, services for ethnic minorities, homes for alcoholics, women's refuges, advice centres, and so on. There is a variety of reasons why voluntary provision of this sort may be more appropriate than statutory. It may permit more involvement of and responsiveness to the intended beneficiaries of services. An independent body may offer a better way of helping minorities whose needs are not recognised by the wider society as legitimate objects for statutory attention and who themselves are suspicious of conventional statutory services. And there may in the voluntary sector be more scope for the expression of strong personal commitments and for ways of working that are flexible and informal. There is also evidence that services provided by voluntary organisations operating in this less bureaucratic manner may cost less than equivalent statutory services. This is quite apart from any cost advantages that may result from the use of volunteers (Hadley *et al.*, 1975, pp. 222–4; Hatch and Mocroft, 1979).

In the eyes of some people the organisations so far discussed are not truly voluntary, in that their work is not carried out mainly by volunteers. But if one reviews what the voluntary sector actually consists of in any particular locality, one finds that it is predominantly composed of a multitude of organisations that do depend on voluntary effort, sometimes backed up by a paid organiser or administrator. Many of these volunteer-run organisations provide services for others, whether by way of meals on wheels, hospital visiting, neighbourhood care schemes, or activities for specific groups like the blind, the mentally handicapped, and so on. In addition, mostly at the informal end of the voluntary spectrum, there is a growing number of organisations that operate mainly on a self-help or mutual aid basis. Thus there are groups for the parents of handicapped children, for people who have to live with specific handicaps or chronic diseases, for single parents, for those with psychiatric problems, and so on. In most cases these are groups for people with a problem that sets them apart from everybody else: but not always, since perhaps the most widespread form of mutual aid relevant to the social services is the playgroup movement.

Altogether this array of voluntary organisations constitutes a substantial and indispensable element in the overall pattern of community care. In addition it is significant that in one field where there is a fast-rising demand — that of advice and counselling — the voluntary sector is the main provider of services. The Citizens Advice Bureaux, Samaritans and Marriage Guidance provide nationwide services, supplemented by numbers of local services usually directed towards specific groups such as young people or those with housing problems. So far the discussion has concentrated on voluntary organisations whose work is in the field of the personal social services and health. The education service is overwhelmingly a statutory one, except in relation to provision for youth where the voluntary sector has a major role, usually one quite well integrated with the statutory services. Income support too is essentially a statutory service, with the voluntary sector playing two rather different roles: on the one hand there are the ancient charities and benevolent funds largely left over from the days before the establishment of the welfare state, and on the other hand are the much more recent pressure groups like the CPAG.

Evidence from the General Household Survey, 1977, and the National Opinion Poll (Hatch, 1978) indicates that some 10 per cent of the population claim they take part in voluntary work on a fairly regular basis. The Wolfenden Committee estimated that in terms of man-hours the voluntary effort directed towards children, the elderly and the handicapped was roughly equivalent in terms of man-hours to that provided by statutory workers in SSDs. However, a considerable proportion of the voluntary effort is absorbed by organisational maintenance — that is, fund-raising, sitting on committees, and so on. On the other hand the paid staff employed by voluntary organisations also need to be included in the picture. They amount to a number equal to about 15 per cent of the staff employed by SSDs.

Thus in quantitative terms the voluntary sector makes a

substantial addition to the resources available for personal social services, but only a small one to health and education, and an almost negligible one to income support. In housing the situation is rather different. There the voluntary work component is very small; but in the past decade central government has made a deliberate decision to develop a more plural pattern of provision. Instead of relying almost exclusively on local authorities to provide rented accommodation, substantial resources have been directed through the Housing Corporation to housing associations. These now account for some 20 per cent of the production of new and converted dwellings for letting. Most accommodation provided by housing associations conforms closely to the standards set for local authorities and is managed in a conventional way. However, within the voluntary field a number of housing co-operatives have come into existence, and the flexibility of some housing associations has enabled them to make a special contribution in accommodating groups with unorthodox needs, such as the single homeless.

One can sum up the positive aspects of the voluntary sector in the following way. It provides a vehicle for the involvement of a substantial minority of the population in caring for each other and in promoting the welfare of their communities. The forms of this involvement and the organisations through which it takes place are numerous and varied. They provide channels for the expression of strong individual commitments, for a more diffuse willingness to help and for doing something about the problems directly experienced by individuals themselves. The sector is a source of new developments, of criticism and pressure, and a medium for taking action where statutory agencies fear to tread. Being smaller and more flexible, with fewer bureaucratic constraints, voluntary organisations can often help in more responsive and personal ways. Evidence about the growth in numbers of organisations suggests that these advantages are becoming more widely recognised. Thus the locality studies carried out for the Wolfenden Committee found that the number of voluntary organisations had risen by 8 per cent in two and a half years, growth being particularly marked among the relatively informal organisations offering mutual aid or neighbourhood care (Hatch, 1980a, ch. 4).

But for all its virtues, in most localities and most fields the voluntary sector is essentially marginal to the statutory sector, in terms both of financial resources and of the way it is treated by the statutory services. Though it receives much public commendation, in practice the voluntary sector is sometimes seen as more of a nuisance than an asset. Thus in terms of grant aid support for the voluntary sector amounts to rather trivial sums – even in the case of SSDs it averages only about 2 per cent of the budget, if one ignores fees paid in respect of individuals in residential institutions run by voluntary organisations (Hatch, 1981). Often enough in SSDs responsibility for relations with voluntary organisations rests with a senior officer with many other calls on his time, supported sometimes by one or two individuals lower down the hierarchy who are expected to enlist volunteers to work directly with the statutory services.

Some local authorities have adopted a more positive approach to the voluntary sector. For example, in one or two SSDs grants to voluntary organisations exceed 10 per cent of the budget. And it is not difficult to envisage a more plural pattern of provision in which other sources of care and services were accorded a much larger role. However, it is important to recognise the obstacles to such a development. Some of them lie with the character of the political and service delivery systems already discussed – unwillingness to relinquish claims to omnicompetence and exclusive legitimacy and to relate to organisations that do not conform to the bureaucratic norms of a large statutory agency. But of course the voluntary sector also has limitations of its own. Put succinctly, it is uneven and unreliable. The propensity to participate in voluntary work is strongly related to social class, so that in areas with only a small proportion of middle-class people there is likely to be less voluntary work and hence, unless perhaps it receives substantial grant aid, a weaker voluntary sector. Similarly, individual voluntary organisations are unevenly spread over the country and one cannot be confident that this spread will correspond to the incidence of the needs with which the organisation is concerned.

Moreover, the commitment of individuals to voluntary organisations is often idiosyncratic and specific. More abstract notions of equity and coverage that are in the forefront for those concerned with social planning are unlikely to animate the volunteer or the self-help group. Thus voluntary organisations are notoriously reluctant to come together in pursuit of wider goals, and the very number of them, let alone their non-bureaucratic *modus operandi*, makes it difficult to know what they do and how well they do it or to remedy deficiencies in their work. Such characteristics often lead to complaints about lack of accountability; but in a more general sense the essential problem is that voluntary organisations are difficult vehicles through which to aim at a broad policy objective and provide universally available services of specified standards.

But these are arguments against exclusive reliance on the voluntary sector, rather than against a plural pattern of provision existing within a framework established by the statutory authorities. What needs to be considered is whether the unreliability and unevenness of the presently fragmented and marginal voluntary sector in this country can be overcome without it assuming the negative bureaucratic features of the statutory system.

The commercial sector

The extent to which social services are provided on a commercial basis, that is, in return for payments by the consumer, varies widely from one service to another. In health and in education, where the role of the commercial sector is most controversial, its contribution is smallest. Thus expenditure on private hospital care, both that provided inside NHS hospitals and that in independent hospitals, has been estimated at £134m. in 1976 (Lee, 1978), or some 3 per cent of NHS expenditure on the hospital service; while in education independent schools accounted for 4 per cent of all pupils and 7 per cent of all teachers in 1977 in England and Wales (*Statistics of Education 1978*, Vol. 1).

In housing the role of the commercial sector is, of course, much greater: a majority of households are owner-occupiers, while private tenants still number one in seven of all households. The field of income support, too, is one where there is a not insignificant private sector. For example, while half the income of pensioner households comes from social security, one-eighth of it is derived from private pension schemes (Family Expenditure Survey, 1977).

In the personal social services the commercial sector is most prominent in the provision of residential care. Thus in England about one in seven of the elderly in residential care are in private homes (*Health and Personal Social Services Statistics 1978*). However, in this field the line between voluntary and commercial provision is particularly difficult to draw, there being a variety of profit-making and non-profit-making establishments dependent in varying degrees upon private fees and charitable giving.

There are certain advantages over statutory provision which the commercial sector shares with the voluntary, such as flexibility, diversity and responsiveness to consumer demand. It can add to the resources available, and being subject to competitive pressures, can offer a source of salutory cost comparisons. Its limitations are summed up in the dictum used by Beveridge that 'The business motive is a good servant but a bad master' (Beveridge, 1948, p. 322). Access to commercially provided services depends upon ability to pay, rather than need. Thus whereas in the NHS the person adjudged to be of low priority will have to join a long waiting list, in the commercial sector if he can pay he can be treated straight away. Some private schools similarly offer advantages which are not available to those educated within the statutory sector.

Another fundamental criticism of commercial provision relates to the effect of the profit motive on the character of the service provided. The providers of any service are likely to be animated by a mixture of motives, some essentially self-regarding, others more altruistic. But there is a particular risk, well illustrated by Titmuss's account of the blood donation service, that the pursuit of profit may reduce the quality of services and lead to the exploitation particularly of individuals with less knowledge and less purchasing power. The concluding passage of the study deserves to be reproduced in full (Titmuss, 1970, pp. 245–6):

From our study of the private market in blood in the United States we have concluded that the commercialisation of blood and donor relationships represses the expression of altruism, erodes the sense of community, lowers scientific standards, limits both personal and professional freedoms, sanctions the making of profits in hospitals and clinical laboratories, legalises hostility between doctor and patient, subjects critical areas of medicine to the laws of the marketplace, places immense social costs on those least able to bear them − the poor, the sick and the inept − increases the danger of unethical behaviour in various sectors of medical science and practice, and results in situations in which proportionately more and more blood is supplied by the poor, the unskilled, the unemployed, Negroes and other low income groups and categories of exploited human populations of high blood yielders. Redistribution in terms of blood and blood products from the poor to the rich appears to be one of the dominant effects of the American blood banking systems.

Moreover, on four testable non-ethical criteria the

commercialised blood market is bad. In terms of economic efficiency it is highly wasteful of blood; shortages, chronic and acute, characterise the demand and supply position and make illusory the concept of equilibrium. It is administratively inefficient and results in more bureaucratisation and much greater administrative, accounting and computer overheads. In terms of price per unit of blood to the patient (or consumer) it is a system which is five to fifteen times more costly than the voluntary system in Britain. And, finally, in terms of quality, commercial markets are much more likely to distribute contaminated blood; the risks for the patient of disease and death are substantially greater. Freedom from disability is inseparable from altruism.

Not all commercial services warrant the same scathing criticism. None the less, on the grounds both of how services are allocated and of standards of provision there is an antithesis between social services and commercial services. A system of social services dominated by the commercial sector thus in important respects negates some of the objectives for which the social services are established. Hence the criticisms levelled at the statutory services in this book should not be taken as arguments for patterns of provision that are predominantly commercial. But there are likely to be situations in which commercial provision, when subject to safeguards to maintain the quality of service and when it does not have a detrimental effect on other sources of service, can contribute usefully to a plural system of services.

Conclusions

The essential point that emerges from this brief review of the informal, voluntary and commercial sectors is that a substantial proportion of all care and services comes from sources other than the state. Yet the statutory services often act in isolation from other sources of care and behave as if they were at the centre of the caring universe. It is also clear that each of the various sources of care has its limitations, as also its strengths, and that none of them stands alone as a single answer to the problems of need and deprivation.

Since the war discussion about the relative roles of the different sectors has centred on the place of commercial as opposed to statutory services. Thus it has been subsumed under the much-debated argument about freedom and equality, and the possibilities of a wider and more sensitive approach have, so to speak, been trampled underfoot in the class struggle. Yet what seems to be needed now is a pluralist strategy which looks beyond the conflict over the commercial sector and seeks to develop roles for each of the sectors and, in particular, to maximise the voluntary and informal contributions. The instrument for formulating a strategy must necessarily be the state, and the statutory sector must provide a framework through which priorities and standards can be maintained. The elements of such a pluralist strategy we examine in the last four chapters. It remains to ask first how suitable our present political institutions are for implementing it.

CHAPTER 7

Representative Democracy

Britain's present system of government can be described as representative democracy. It evolved during the nineteenth century out of the oligarchic government of the eighteenth century, as increasing numbers of people obtained the vote. By the early years of the twentieth century, the political parties, Parliament, Cabinet government and local councils had taken a form which has changed surprisingly little since then. But though the political forms remain the same, during the present century the responsibilities of government have extended out of all recognition. Thus largely unchanged political institutions now preside over an administrative system that has grown many times over.

Under this system the essential link between the people and the state is the political parties. They put forward to the electorate a choice of representatives and programmes, and the process of choosing between the parties serves to influence and legitimise the system. Moreover, at any rate in theory, membership of the political parties offers wide opportunities for closer involvement to the more committed or public-spirited. During recent years the role of the parties has waxed rather than waned: in particular, since local government reorganisation there are now few local authorities where anyone not sponsored by one of the main parties has much chance of being elected.

Given this key role, one might have expected that, as the responsibilities of the state expanded, more and more people would have been drawn into active membership of the parties. But in fact the opposite is true. The clearest evidence of declining involvement comes from the Labour Party. Despite its strong democratic, populist tradition the number of individual members of the Labour Party is now only about a quarter of its peak figure of 1 million in 1950; and the active participants in party affairs have become a dwindling band (Fabian Society, 1980). This makes local branches of the party susceptible to takeover by organised minorities, and means that the number of people involved in the key function of selecting candidates for elections is very small.

What has happened is that, as far as the mass of the voters is concerned, the party struggle has turned into a contest between the national leaders conducted through the national media. It is this, together of course with the actual actions of national government, that influences how people vote, to the exclusion of local events and activities. Voters do exercise a choice between the main parties at general elections: they also use local elections, like national by-elections, to pass interim verdicts on the national government. But the result is that because of this nationalisation of party politics, the representative system as it now operates does not give the mass of the population the chance to express a verdict on the activities of its local politicians. An analysis of ward voting which sought to overturn the conventional view that the results of local elections are determined by national issues indicated that about 75 per cent of the swing between local elections was indeed attributable to national factors. Of the remaining 25 per cent, only a small part resulted from city-wide as opposed to ward factors (Green, 1972). Yet paradoxically, what local election campaigns are usually directed at are the city-wide issues which have the least influence on the voters. Also paradoxically, the tendency for local politicians to believe that their actions have much more influence on the voters than is actually the case may make them behave more responsively than the realities of the situation would warrant. Thus the local representative machinery is not entirely meaningless. Nevertheless it falls far short of the model derived from national politics.

Up to a point this is a realistic response to the high level of centralisation of government in Britain. But it has significant consequences in that it leaves the key decisions as to who represents an area to small caucuses of party activists. Under a system of representative democracy the legitimacy of government rests on the verdict of the electors. But once a local election has ceased to be a verdict on local politicians, with what justice can the latter claim legitimacy from it? Despite the weak answers local politicians are bound to give to this question, they continue to argue that they alone represent the people.

Nor is it just a matter of legitimacy. The implications of the situation become more evident when related to the analyses in other chapters of the development of professionalisation and bureaucracy. The large systems established to deliver services develop an impetus of their own, and are difficult for local politicians to understand fully, let alone control. A local representative system does act as a safety valve for complaints and discontent, but altogether it is only a tenuous way of linking the people with the state.

Although, as shown in Chapter 3, politicians not infrequently complain that they cannot control the system of which they are the nominal masters, the logic of the system tends to make it ever more extensive and uncontrollable. The competition for support means that politicians are always needing to make claims as to what they have achieved. Whether this is a matter of making more services available or of rectifying things that have gone wrong with existing services, politicians have to be seen to be doing something. One consequence, discussed in Chapter 5, is the desire to implement changes before the next election. Another is that decisions have to be taken at a high level in the authority. In order for this to happen discretion is taken away from the local level: instead information is passed up from the local level, filtered at each level of the hierarchy, and eventually used for making decisions at the top. This tendency was intensified by the larger scale of local government resulting from the 1974 reorganisation. It is also all the time being reinforced by crises, since whenever these occur there is pressure to take decisions to a higher level in the machine and, as part of the solution, to define the roles of those lower down more precisely and narrowly.

Of course this does not mean that people low in the hierarchy who know their local situation are necessarily in the right; or that they should be made less accountable. The point is that if they are to be made accountable, it ought to be at a local level to people who know about their work, are affected by it and might co-operate with them in carrying it out. But this is not possible in a representative system which accords legitimacy exclusively to the products of the electoral system described above. For them devolved responsibility and a sharing of accountability has nothing to commend it. The logic of their situation leads them rather to develop bureaucracies oriented upwards, away from the people they are supposed to be serving.

From time to time there are tensions between the politicians and the administrators and professionals who run these bureaucracies. But basically the upwards-oriented bureaucracy suits the latter as well as the former, since it frees them from interference by the consumers of their services and offers attractive ladders up which to advance careers. Thus, even though the politicians have not confined their own roles to policy-making in the way the organisational reformers discussed in Chapter 5 hoped, representative democracy is highly congruent with the kinds of organisation that emerged from those reforms. Conversely, and this is a crucial point for the present discussion, it is not congruent with more participative and community-oriented forms of social service provision.

Any critique of democratic institutions requires a clear understanding of what sort of democracy one is talking about. Underlying most discussions of democracy in Western countries are two different views as to what it consists of. The distinction between them is developed by C. B. MacPherson in *The Life and Times of Liberal Democracy* (1977). One he identifies as the equilibrium or pluralist elitist model. The essence of this model (p. 78) is that:

> Democracy is simply a mechanism for choosing and authorising governments, not a kind of society nor a set of moral ends; . . . the mechanism consists of a competition between two or more self-chosen sets of politicians (elites), arrayed in political parties, for the votes which will entitle them to rule until the next election . . . the voters in choosing between parties register their desire for one batch of political goods rather than another. The purveyors of the batch which gets the most votes become the authorised rulers until the next election: they cannot tyrannise because there will be a next election.

This model, MacPherson argues, is a reasonably accurate description of how Western political systems do in fact operate. It does not allow for pressure groups, and in some contexts one might prefer to describe politicians as caucus-chosen rather than self-chosen. Nevertheless, the model does convey the limited nature of popular involvement in national politics. But in local politics, for the reasons explained above, the choice presented to the citizen has even less reality.

The alternative for which MacPherson argues is participatory democracy. This cannot be described or defined on the basis of existing practice. But in essence it rests on critiques of pluralist elitism and upon more positive beliefs in the ability of ordinary citizens to define issues, decide and act for themselves and in so doing to achieve a measure of self-realisation and fulfilment. We return to it in the next part of the book. Here it is necessary to draw together the threads of our critique of the present system.

From the end of the war until recently the present system managed to stimulate and satisfy a high level of consumer demand. Pluralist democracy indeed sat happily with the affluent worker, that archetypal figure of postwar society delineated by the researchers from Cambridge University (Goldthorpe *et al.*, 1968a, 1968b, 1969). It may be that the workers of Luton, who provided the basis for their study, were not as archetypal as the researchers argued, in that they were drawn disproportionately from the kind of people who especially wanted higher earnings. Nevertheless, the affluent worker is a figure, indeed a phenomenon, who serves to elucidate and underline a number of the essential features of the social system that brought prosperity and stability to Britain during the third quarter of the century.

Perhaps the most essential feature of this system was increasing prosperity. For all the inadequacy of Britain's economic performance when compared to other non-communist industrial and industrialising nations, it produced both extra money for people to spend and sufficient resources to permit a large growth of the social services. All this meant that there was more for nearly everyone, and that competitions for resources could be resolved without there having to be a loser. Another related feature of the system was the emphasis on the acquisition of consumer goods – homes, cars and durables for use in the home. These were conducive to a home-centred, family-oriented life, which valued jobs, trades unions and political parties not for inherent virtues of their own, but rather as a means of acquiring consumer goods.

Taking a cynical view, one could say one was witnessing a latter-day counterpart of the bread and circuses of the Roman emperors. Less cynically, the middle mass of the population was for the first time in history enjoying a material standard of living hitherto reserved only for an upper crust. Moreover it was enjoying this emancipation under a regime that assured it civil liberties and did offer it at least a limited influence over its rulers and the policies they adopted. If this was social democracy it had substantial virtues.

The political system under which these developments took place has rested upon competition between elites. This gives a premium to dramatising and simplifying the issues, to synthesising big problems and big solutions out of the shreds and tatters of everyday life, and to carrying over into the implementation of welfare programmes the gestures of the public debate. But it is a feature of representative democracy as practised in Western countries nowadays that it provides roles for only a handful of actors, while yet impinging to an ever greater extent on the lives of its citizens.

It was not, we would suggest, entirely fortuitous or as a result of a peculiar combination of stupidity, incompetence, or malevolence that things have come about in this way. The conjunction of representative democracy, with its handful of actors bidding for the endorsement of millions of intermittently interested spectators, and an already pervasive and extensive state, directs aspirations towards statutory action, creates expectations of what the state can achieve and sucks more and more people into the statutory apparatus. Yet the hierarchies that separate the decision-makers from the needs and the problems, the necessity of cranking up cumbrous bureaucratic machinery and buying off vested interests within the machinery, all mean that the state in its present form will be an ineffective and expensive instrument for meeting those aspirations and expectations. These are some of the factors underlying the present crisis of the social democratic state.

CHAPTER 8

After Social Democracy

That there is a crisis of the social democratic state was the theme with which the last chapter ended. We argued that the prosperous and stable character of Britain during the third quarter of the century depended on a set of interrelated factors – increasing production, a predominantly home-centred and consumption-oriented populace, the ability of the state to provide an increasing volume of social services and a form of non-participatory representative democracy. But a number of assumptions and understandings that have underpinned the postwar social democratic state are ceasing to hold good. Our attention has been directed mainly to the social services. In this field we have argued that there is a self-defeating character to much of the bold statutory activity of recent years. Results produced by it are limited, largely because of the centralised, non-participatory character of the systems that were brought into existence to meet needs many of which were of their essence idiosyncratic, specific and personal.

To recapitulate, we have shown how substantial increases in spending by the state on the social services over the last two decades have failed to result in anything approaching proportionate returns in benefits to the community; how statutory policies have grossly underestimated the importance of the contribution of the informal and voluntary sectors and their potential for development; and yet how the faith of the establishment in traditional centralist solutions to current problems has remained unshaken, in spite of the accumulation of evidence of their inadequacy. The relationship of the social services to the system of representative government and its administrative apparatus has also been explored and we have shown why this system is fundamentally incompatible with any radical strategy to increase the effectiveness of the services through participatory policies.

But it is in other fields that the postwar settlement seems to be even more obviously and critically under strain. In particular, since the oil crisis the rate of economic growth has dropped in Britain almost to zero. There is no longer the wherewithal to finance extensions to social services and to give everyone a bit extra. Competition for resources instead takes on the character of a zero-sum game in which gains are made only at the expense of other parties. Thus social conflict is translated into inflation, which seems paradoxically conjoined with unemployment. Hence the growing problems with which government seems unable to cope.

Moreover, these problems are not just temporary ones which will go away and let things get back to normal sooner or later. For example, it could be argued that higher oil prices require an adjustment to world trade, and that once this has been made, economic growth will be resumed as before. However, the oil crisis is a special case of a more general phenomenon, the exhaustion of material resources. In future the real cost of energy and raw materials is likely to rise instead of declining, and thus to absorb more of the results of the improvements of productivity that would otherwise have been released for consumption. There has also been a secular change in expectations of the state and institutional behaviour towards it. Whereas in the past relatively minor adjustments in the level of demand in the economy served to reduce the rate of inflation, today much larger reductions in demand and twice the rate of unemployment prevalent twenty years ago seem to have very little effect. The point is that the bargaining power of organised labour and of the other corporate interests has become too strong for what were once thought of as immutable economic laws. This promises to be as true of the economic laws resuscitated by the monetarists as of the ones embodied in Keynesian doctrines.

Thus in a variety of ways the state is becoming the object of expectations which it cannot satisfy, and there is a similar range of reasons why changes seem to be required that would alter in a fundamental way the rules and assumptions that have provided the foundations for the social democratic state. Consequently we have entered an era of flux. The old governing assumptions will not do, but what the new ones will be is not clear. Britain is not unique in this respect. Other Western industrial societies are in a similar position. But because Britain was the first to industrialise and because it is the society in which the social democratic state is most clearly breaking down, it may be nearer to a turning point than any other country.

There are two obvious and widely canvassed directions of change; in the view of the traditional left the answer is to increase the power of the state; while for the right the answer is to lower expectations and to reduce the role of the state in favour of private enterprise. Although the reasons for rejecting both answers are probably evident from the arguments already advanced, it is important to make the objections to each absolutely clear.

In the case of the conventional left or state socialist approach, the solution represents an intensification of the problems rather than an answer to them. State socialists nowadays readily pay tribute to participation, but the essential thrust of their policies for social welfare are for more of the existing kinds of services, combined with steps to curtail the private sector and either indifference or distrust towards informal and voluntary action. The state socialists would extend and strengthen the existing structures of the state, and by democratic control usually mean party or trade union control. The organised left in Britain, in both its militant and less militant forms, is increasingly a movement of *petits fonctionnaires*, who equate progress with the creation of greater roles for themselves and the organisations they work for.

The answer of the right, like that of the left, represents an attempt to apply old solutions to new problems, though in the case of the right it seems to be the 1920s instead of the 1940s that provides the paradigms. In terms of social welfare the solutions currently advocated by the right are inimical not only to the overdeveloped state but to collective provision of all kinds. Characteristic of this tendency is the defence of the private market in blood attacked by Titmuss. Perhaps the main point is that the notion of wider involvement in welfare provision can have only a token value in the absence of a redistributory state framework and a mixture of public and voluntary organisations through which involvement can be realised.

If these solutions are the most widely canvassed response to the present *impasse*, they are not widely popular. There is an ambivalence about the role of the state along the left–right political continuum. Thus there has always been a strong element in the Conservative Party which believed in benevolent paternalism, and it is not yet extinct. Similarly on the left, ever since the conflict be-tween Marx and Bakunin at the First International, there has been tension between libertarianism and *étatisme*, though with *étatisme*, either in its social democratic or in its Marxist guise, generally in the ascendant. Thus in arguing for a third alternative to the conventional answers to the problems of our time one is not arguing for a midway compromise between the existing poles, but for something new, for movement along a different dimension from the one which has been the main battleground of institutionalised conflict. There are signs of this new direction of development in the arguments that have been advanced for what has been called market socialism, in the 'small is beautiful' approach to economic organisation, in the advocacy of intermediate or appropriate technology, in some expressions of the growing interest in voluntary action (Wolfenden, 1977; Gladstone, 1979) and in a variety of experiments in alternative patterns of living. Thus there is a common element in many of the critiques being advanced of modern industrialised societies and in the alternative solutions with which people are beginning to grapple. They point towards a pattern for future development radically different from that predominant since the war.

Unfortunately most thinking about the future that stems from this alternative perspective is still articulating yearnings rather than presenting a strategy for the future. The intellectual task of giving coherence and form to these yearnings remains to be done. The remaining chapters seek to contribute to the carrying out of this task. A starting point is alternative forms of social service provision already in existence. Descriptions of these form the substance of Chapter 9. But at present they are isolated and untypical and coexist uneasily with the dominant institutions. How therefore can structures be created that would be conducive to a more participative and decentralised form of service provision? This is the question discussed in Chapter 10. Finally, Chapter 11 seeks to relate alternative strategies for the social services to a wider set of social and political issues. It argues that a number of common themes are emerging which promise to form the core of a new radicalism.

CHAPTER 9

Theory into Practice

Outside the cloistered world of the academic, ideas have little authority if they cannot be demonstrated to be practical or practicable. Much of the strength of the case for decentralisation and for the evolutionary development of public involvement in social service provision lies in the growing evidence that on a modest scale it is already taking place, and that where it is found it usually leads to marked improvements in the services concerned. In this chapter we review a sample of such developments, drawn to illustrate the range of services covered and the variety of methods through which involvement has been widened.

They fall broadly into two categories. On the one hand are arrangements for decentralising statutory services. These place the main emphasis on changes in the methods of working of the staff of statutory agencies, creating both structures that make for responsiveness to the community and the consumer and democratic forms of decision-making within the organisation. On the other hand are developments best described as pluralism. Pluralism can have various meanings. What it signifies here are the ideas that social services can come from a variety of sources, not just from staff directly employed by government, and that for numerous reasons it is desirable to maximise the involvement in care and service provision of people outside the statutory agencies. In essence, therefore, what follow are illustrations of a two-pronged strategy for decentralisation and pluralism.

The non-statutory sources of social service have been reviewed in Chapter 6 and their potential in contributing to the development of pluralism has been sufficiently indicated there, and in the sources mentioned, to make any general elaboration of the theme unnecessary in this chapter. We begin this chapter with descriptions of two kinds of voluntary initiatives that are perhaps less well known: first, local generalist bodies set up to encourage voluntary action at neighbourhood level; secondly, two schemes established to support self-help amongst disadvantaged groups in society.

While the role of the voluntary sector in the development of a pluralist strategy is quite readily established, it is more difficult to contend that statutory services might act in a community-oriented way, decentralising their own organisations and encouraging the development of voluntary initiatives. The main focus of this chapter, therefore, is on innovation in the statutory services. The examples are arranged according to field of activity, beginning with health, followed by education and the personal social services. Implicit in most of these examples is a model of service delivery that departs in certain fundamental ways from the conventional one. The chapter ends by using the case of SSD area teams to identify key elements of the two models.

The schemes described here vary considerably in form and scope. Likewise, as must be expected in an innovative field of this kind, the accounts on which these short descriptions are based are uneven in their depth and authority. Nevertheless, it is a common feature that those responsible for running the schemes perceive the public involved as more than passive consumers. Whether their formal contact with the organisation is as user, client, relative, neighbour, or friend of client, the public are seen by the staff of the organisation as a resource, people who can and should be invited to play an active part in the provision of the service and in enhancing its scope and quality.

Neighbourhood councils and centres

Much, perhaps most, voluntary action is highly specific in its goals and organisation. Typically, voluntary bodies are formed to pursue a particular end and their members have little interest in the wider implications of voluntarism or the notion of a general voluntary movement. Critics of the voluntary sector are likely to point to this narrowness of focus as a weakness, a tendency which will always block progress towards the development of a more significant role for the sector in planning and policy-making. There have, of course, been some longstanding exceptions at local level to such tunnel vision, settlements and councils of voluntary service being the most obvious examples. But in recent years there has been a significant growth of generalist bodies of new kinds concerned with the wider development of voluntary action at local level. Neighbourhood councils and centres are probably the most important examples of such bodies. Below we briefly describe two of these organisations which are currently operating in London. Both schemes involve the creation of a physical and organisational context for the development of a range of local voluntary activities. Both illustrate how, when such a context can be provided, new sources of voluntary action can be tapped at neighbourhood level, even in 'deprived' inner city areas.

The account of the first scheme, a community centre in Islington, is based on a forthcoming report on voluntary–statutory relationships in two local authorities (Mocroft and Hatch, forthcoming).

The Factory

The establishment of the 'Factory' community centre in Newington Green in 1974 owes its origins to the development of an explicit 'public participation policy' to increase the community's say in the running and direction of council services. This in turn led to the use of voluntary organisations as vehicles for 'participation' and to the expansion of community work in order to encourage, develop and spread voluntary organisations in the borough. A community worker placed in the Newington Green area and charged with the development of a participatory, neighbourhood forum found that the immediate demand from people in the area was for a community centre as a base for a range of activities.

The existence of a small disused factory – acquired by the council as part of a road-widening scheme which subsequently fell through – offered the opportunity of establishing a permanent home for the various local projects which were just getting under way. An Urban Aid application for a community centre with a revenue budget of £23,000 was quickly agreed and a steering committee of local people was set up. Many of these 'locals', however, already had some professional interest in social or community work. A full-time worker was appointed and the project was publicised in the area by leaflets and public meetings. Several projects were able to start operating soon after the building was obtained, including the first mother and toddler club in the area which was suggested by a local resident who lived near The Factory and is still involved in its running six years later. Another local woman managed to stir up interest in playschemes, especially after-school schemes which could help working mothers. This woman has now become a paid part-time youth worker at The Factory. Yet another proposal from local residents was a toy library; and from the local social services area team came a proposal for one of Islington's childminders' centres. The Factory was lucky in that there were several schemes like these already proposed or getting under way and looking for premises, so it could take them under its wing and thereby have a good base of services to justify its existence at an early stage.

The core staff of The Factory (not including paid sessional play leaders and youth leaders) today consists of four people: a full-time community worker, a full-time youth worker and two part-timers – an under-5s worker and an administrative assistant. Current projects include an ILEA youth club, holiday playschemes, holiday arrangements for families and children, a food co-operative, the Early Morning Club for families with mothers who go to work well before school starts, a pensioners' lunch club, the childminders' centre, the mother and toddler club, craftwork classes and English classes for immigrants funded by outside bodies (both of these last two have creche facilities provided from The Factory's core funding, without which they could not continue).

As well as Urban Aid and social services committee grants, The Factory has received support from other bodies, including Neighbourhood English Classes, a local religious body, ILEA adult education, ILEA youth service and the local social services team project funds. The Factory was fortunate in being able to capitalise on ILEA's keenness to develop youth services in the area. In return for basic premises in an already thriving community centre, ILEA spent £30,000 on modernising the basement – the last unused part of the building – and seconds sessional youth leaders to The Factory. Thus The Factory provides an example of an Urban Aid grant securing disused premises which can offer a cheap base for locally run services: a purpose-built youth club would certainly have cost ILEA far more than its initial outlay of £30,000. The Hackney and Islington Inner City Partnership scheme is another example of the luck which has shone on The Factory throughout its life; indeed it almost seemed designed as a source of funding for The Factory. It enabled the project to regularise its position as a local provider of services on the very edge of Islington Borough. Many of its users are Hackney residents so Partnership funding was able to clear up an anomalous position whereby Islington expenditure benefited

Hackney residents. Contact with the local social services area team
was also fruitful: their team projects activities helped to establish the
pensioners' lunch club. Contact with the local community is
maintained in a number of ways: directly through staff talking to
individual mothers, pensioners, childminders, and so on; by
employing local mothers as paid sessional playgroup workers; and
through the management body, the users' committee. This has no
formal councillor or officer representation but consists of fourteen
people (plus the staff) divided about equally between interested locals
and representatives of the various groups who use the building.

The Telegraph Hill Neighbourhood Council

This neighbourhood council had its origins at the beginning of the
1970s when part of a large neo-Gothic church in the Telegraph Hill
area of New Cross was converted into a community centre. An
executive committee, the representatives from many different
activities for all age-groups in the local community, was set up. This
formed the basis of the neighbourhood council. From the beginning the project was able to attract outside funding as well as
local money. Today its sponsors include both the local council and
ILEA.

The area covered by the neighbourhood council is a mixed one,
including a high proportion of local authority housing, some
ownership-occupied dwellings and some private rented
accommodation in the multiple occupancy. 'The population is
mixed both in colour and socio-economic groupings. About a
quarter of the residents of Telegraph Hill are black. The area is not
one of obvious deprivation and poverty, but it suffers from gross
neglect of many houses, and the lack of many amenities' (Pennock,
1980, p. 36).

Today anyone who lives in New Cross or Brockley is
automatically a member of the neighourhood council and is entitled
to vote at the AGM. The AGM elects the officers and ten members
of the executive, as well as approving policies for the coming year:

The Executive meets monthly and consists of elected members,
representatives of sub-committees and representatives of all
affiliated organisations. The meetings are open to anyone. The
Executive attempts to look at not only the business of the
Neighbourhood Council but also the concerns of affiliated groups,
and wider issues that affect the area. (Pennock, 1980, p. 36)

The neighbourhood centre has been built on to the end of the church. It has a large meeting room with a stage, a lounge and bar, a coffee bar, a youth hall and a number of smaller rooms. Its paid staff include a warden, a youth worker, an old people's organiser, a caretaker and secretaries. The centre hosts a wide range of activities among which are a youth club, an old people's day centre, playgroups and mother and toddler groups. In the evenings the centre is used by many recreational groups.

The council has rented a shop as an office and base for its community development work. Three paid community workers are located there and help to promote and encourage locality based groups, particularly local residents' and tenants' associations. The council produces its own community newspaper which has a readership of about 5,000. Two secretaries/advisers are available in the office to give help and advice, to arrange for expert legal advice, and to provide office resources for local voluntary groups.

Some of the initiatives sponsored through the council and centre over the last two years include (Pennock, 1980, p. 35):

Groups working on traffic problems in the area, disputing local government proposals and proposing alternative schemes.

A group which has taken up the whole question of repairs and maintenance of council estates, and another looking at the kind of pressure needed to ensure that tenants are not exploited by private landlords.

A number of people who have got together to examine the implications of the Taylor Report for the running of the local schools.

The most ambitious development has been the sponsoring of a co-operative clothing factory and workshop complex to help relieve unemployment in the area. This scheme, which is backed by local council funding, is expected to employ more than seventy people.

Self-help groups and a self-help centre

In recent years there has been a rapid expansion of self-help groups amongst those suffering from forms of physical and mental illness, and socially defined problems such as homosexuality. These groups can bring a great deal of support and help to their members but their structures are often fragile and their functions and potentials are frequently not well understood by professionals operating in the fields concerned.

Jane Mellett worked closely with a number of such groups in Nottingham, mainly in the mental health field. Her early experiences of two groups, phobics and depressives, showed her the risk that the professional worker can run of becoming too deeply involved and so making the groups dependent on him or her and preventing them from developing their own resources. But she also recognised the importance of remaining available as a resource to the group, when advice or intervention with other agencies on its behalf might be required. And she believed the groups should be freed as far as possible from the practical burdens of finding and financing their own premises for meetings and activities. One group she was working with, Depressives Anonymous, was having great difficulty in maintaining a centre it had opened and was in danger of collapse as a result. This led Jane Mellett to encourage the local mental health association to take over the tenancy of the premises and operate them as a self-help centre (Mellett, 1980, p. 28):

> The Self-help Centre, being quite distinct from any one group, was able to attract funds in its own right. Different groups were asked if they would like to make use of the premises, which thus came to be used by four different A.A. groups, Al Anon, Gamblers Anonymous and Gam Anon, and D.A. Each of these groups meets at a different time and has complete control over the premises for that time. They have two small meeting rooms and facilities for making coffee for £1·80 a week. They can spend all evening or afternoon in the Centre, drinking as much tea and coffee as they wish to consume. The rents are collected by the Centre's treasurer who was appointed by the Mental Health Association, and he is responsible for paying all bills. The daily management of the Centre is carried out by the secretary of the management group, formerly myself. The management group meets about four times a year to discuss the facilities of the Centre, with representatives from each group present. We found that through meeting at the same Centre, groups come into contact with each other more often. Some individuals would go around several of the meetings in order to find the one that suited them best, and because the premises were the same and there was only one group meeting at a time, it was not confusing for individuals

to find the meetings. In some instances it was possible for an individual to go to two or more meetings of different groups each week. In addition to this movement of individuals between the groups, the groups themselves have gained support and encouragement from each other, which has allowed them to preserve and continue meetings without feeling isolated. They are part of a larger body of self-help groups and are able to place the emphasis of their meetings on the needs of their individual members rather than on the organisation of premises. The burden of administration on myself and the treasurer was really very small as we were not concerned with the detailed happenings within each group, but rather with their concrete needs. At the same time, I was able to act as a link person between the groups, and as a resource for new groups seeking support and encouragement. This role is a recognised function for staff of the Council for Voluntary Service, but I see no reason why the role could not be played by other professionals, provided they are prepared to limit their involvement and influence on the activities and aims of the groups. The Self-help Centre was purely a resource which was offered to and used by small self-help groups, providing a private meeting place from which a group could gain strength and develop.

Another form of self-help with potentially far-reaching implications is aimed particularly at those who have recently come out of institutional care or custody and are faced with all the problems of coming to terms with life outside. It can be seen as establishing alternative forms of household to those based on the nuclear family.

Patchwork Community Limited

Patchwork has now been in operation for some eight years. It is legally constituted as a charitable housing association and has both permanent property and about a hundred short-life houses. It aims to provide housing for a wide variety of people who wish to live communally. Whilst currently catering mainly for single people, some of whom are simply homeless, others are in more specific need – such as ex-offenders, ex-psychiatric patients, ex-addicts, and so on. Although Patchwork houses a large proportion of people normally classified as in 'special need' it does not employ wardens or social workers as such. Patchwork relies for social support on a high ratio of staff, drawn entirely from residents, and primarily on the informal support of one resident for another. The aim is to provide an element of stability, independence and friendship in the lives of many who have become used to the impermanence and regimentation of institutions. Thus, concentration on any one kind of need in any one household is avoided. So, ideally a household is a mix of people from a variety of backgrounds seeking to develop ways of living together. All Patchwork staff, its workforce, administrative and housing management staff, receive a common wage and must live in Patchwork as a condition of employment.

There are two main types of household. First, a 'Patchwork house' – here Patchwork issues a licence to each individual joining a household: the weekly licence fee (rent) paid by the resident covers a range of services and maintenance costs which are then met centrally by Patchwork. Secondly, there are 'group houses' – such houses are licensed to a group of people who then assume full responsibility for payment of fuel bills, choice of new residents, and so on. In addition, from time to time Patchwork has been able to offer houses to established groups wishing to explore more specialist care for needy individuals and has been able to use its established position as a housing association to support several new initiatives in such specialist provision. Most of Patchwork's housing is in the London area and some in the home counties with, in early 1980, some 500 residents (Reddin, 1980).

Health

Health care has come to be seen by some as the example *par excellence* of professionalism in the social services. Increases in medical knowledge and technology have enhanced the authority of the physician in many parts of the field. Yet at the same time it has become increasingly apparent that many diseases respond poorly to treatment and can only be prevented by self-care, while others are chronic conditions which call for sustained routine care rather than high technology. The need for public involvement in both prevention and care is self-evident, but growing numbers of both service-providers and service-users are now convinced that participation should be on a much broader base and its potential should be considered in every aspect of service delivery.

The schemes described here based on general practice include patients' committees, a scheme for the care of the dying and another embracing more general neighbourhood care of the elderly. In the hospital setting we give accounts of an experiment in democratic ward management, and two attempts to bring hospital services into the home. Outside the health service itself, the self-help centre described earlier is also relevant.

(1) *General Practice*

The Patients' Committee. During the 1970s several general practices in Britain invited their patients to form committees and to participate in the running of the practices. The aims behind one such scheme, set up in a Bristol practice in 1973, are probably fairly typical. Writing to the *Journal of the Royal College of General Practitioners*, Dr T. F. Paine said: 'The provision of medical care in this country is insufficiently democratic, particularly at the grass-roots level of general practice. However well a practice is run, patients have a right to be consulted and to express their opinions and criticisms of it. After all, they pay for it.' The aims of setting up the patients' association in this practice were (Paine, 1974, p. 351):

> to provide the practice community with a voice in the organisation of its general medical care, both at the surgery level (e.g. appointments systems) and at the community levels (e.g. home care for the elderly); to provide effective means of two-way communication between our patients and their doctors, allowing an open airing of views on all relevant subjects, particularly those which are at all controversial, and which may sometimes cause ill-feeling (e.g. difficulties with the appointments system, home visiting policy); to foster discussions of a purely informative nature (e.g. aspects of health education, advances in medicine); to augment, and possibly help in co-ordinating, the existing voluntary services within the community; and lastly, and certainly not least, to help keep the doctors on their toes, and to encourage a continuing process of self – and practice – audit.

Five years later Dr Paine was able to report considerable progress towards the achievement of these aims (Paine, 1979). Between forty and fifty patients had responded to the doctors' initial proposal to establish a group and it had been decided from the start that the group would be run entirely by the patients 'not only to avoid any extra load on the doctors but because it was felt that it was the patients' "thing". As such we should not risk it being too dominated by, or dependent on, any of the doctors.'

The active core of the association is its community care volunteers. These consist of about fifty patients, one of whom acts as the co-ordinator for the group. She produces a twice-yearly circular which lists the volunteers and gives an account of the work of the association. 'The community care system is very straightforward. Someone − doctor, district nurse, or neighbour − realises that a patient needs some help. The co-ordinator . . . is contacted. If she feels the task is reasonable, she goes through her list of volunteers until she finds someone to do the job.'

Volunteers undertake a wide range of activities including regular visits to individual patients to talk, to read to them, to garden and do other jobs. The volunteers run a transport service and can claim 5p a mile towards their car costs from the funds of the association. Every week a group of the volunteers organises lunch for about twenty lonely old people at a local Friends' Meeting House. This group also takes the old people on outings to the theatre and the seaside.

In addition, the association offers advice on welfare rights and a number of volunteers have been active in setting up self-help groups. These include a young mothers' group, a 'giving-up-smoking group' and a yoga group.

While this association was being established in a middle-class area of Bristol, a similar scheme was being planned in working-class Aberdare. A new health centre was opened there in 1973 to serve a population of 10,000. The doctors and other members of the health team decided to set up a patients' committee to share in running the primary care service, to consider complaints and improvements, to provide health education, to communicate patients' opinions to other bodies such as the community health council and the health authority, to improve levels of care and to set up subcommittees to deal with various aspects of patients' needs. The committee meets at least monthly and is attended by members of the health team. Members of the committee and health staff have formed joint deputations to visit the local district management team in attempts to improve services. Medical staff feel they can communicate their problems more effectively to patients and in turn learn more about the patients' points of view. One of the doctors involved, A. J. M. Wilson, notes that considerable emphasis has been placed on pre-ventive medicine, which is considered a high priority in a working-class practice where illness rates are higher but people are traditionally reluctant to ' "bother the doctor" often enough or soon enough. Their death and illness rates are the highest and their lives the shortest. The Patients' Committee aims to encourage people to come early in their illness when so many lives can be saved and so much ameliorative treatment provided' (Wilson, 1977, p. 398).

Action taken to encourage prevention and early treatment has included the establishment of an age action committee, support for a social club for the mentally ill and the sponsorship of numerous lectures and discussions. A synopsis of each lecture is published in the local newspaper. Dr Wilson believes that such measures are helping to create a more educated public

> who, because of their improved understanding, are able to participate in the 'open' form of medicine which is being developed. This means that patient and doctor discuss the probable diagnosis and treatment: why, for example, antibiotics or tranquillisers are not given, or given; and the action and side effects of drugs, etc. The patient is being given the confidence to say to the doctor − 'Why?'

The Aberdare health team also echo Dr Paine's point on the need for greater accountability in the NHS (Wilson, 1977, p. 398):

> The NHS produced the most important advance in health care in this country but it also reduced democratic control over the health service . . . Government policy is one of delegation downwards to health authorities and accountability upwards to the DHSS. Health authorities are appointed, not elected, and so are not accountable to the local people.
>
> The elected patients' committee, on the other hand, is an example of local democracy and accountability from the health team to the people. Doctors have to be accountable. Why not to our patients whom we know?

The number of practices in which patients' committees have been formed has continued to grow and in 1978 several of the groups came together to found the National Association for Patient Participation in General Practice, electing Sir George Godber as their first president. The association aims to provide links between existing patients' groups, provide information for those thinking of starting groups, promote the principles and benefits of patient participation and win official support and encouragement (Paine, 1978, pp. 337–80). Eighteen months after its foundation there were about twenty patients' groups in the association.

Practical care and the General Practice. Several of the patients' groups, in addition to their other activities, act as a means for recruiting voluntary helpers to assist the work of the practice in tasks for patients such as visiting, transport and shopping. In some cases neighbourly services of this kind have been the central purpose in setting up a committee. One example is the scheme established in 1974 in the Glaven area, in north Norfolk, by Dr Allibone. The practice of 2,400 patients had at the time well over the national average of elderly and very elderly. Six hundred were over 65 and 359 of these over 70. A substantial minority lived alone and were dependent on the help of a neighbour. Services for these and other frail elderly were quite inadequate.

Dr Allibone's aim in establishing the Glaven District Caring Scheme was to combine the resources of the twelve villages covered by his practice to create a community caring team. A committee was formed of people already involved in caring as good neighbours in the villages. It was to be the job of its members to identify elderly people in need of help and to link them to the scheme. A smaller executive committee was elected by the main committee to manage the various activities undertaken in the scheme. Today four main services have been established.

Transport. Each village has a list of drivers ready to take old people to the doctor and dentist, and to visit friends and relatives in hospital. Drivers can claim petrol costs from the scheme. Through joint funding it has been possible to buy a minibus with back hoist and this is driven by a team of volunteer drivers.

Luncheon club. A luncheon club has been set up and meals are provided twice weekly for twenty-five elderly people. Transport is provided to and from the club by volunteers.

Day hospital. With the support of the district council the small community centre of a local group housing project has been extended to make a day centre for the elderly. This has a new day room, dining room, kitchen, bathroom and physiotherapy room. Every day ten to fifteen elderly patients are cared for at the centre and some receive physiotherapy and occupational therapy.

Nursing volunteers. About thirty volunteers have received a simple training in home nursing. Under the general supervision of a district nurse and the management of a volunteer, who is a qualified SRN and midwife, the volunteers are allocated to jobs including bathing, foot care, bed-making, helping at the day hospital and, in some cases, a night sitting service.

Thanks to a grant from a trust the scheme has also been able to appoint its own voluntary services organiser. In total, the scheme costs about £3,000 a year to run: £1,300 of this is provided by the social services and the rest is raised by members of the scheme themselves (Bayley, 1978; Allibone, 1979).

Care of the dying. Many, perhaps most, people would prefer to die in the familiar surroundings of their own home, with their families around them, rather than in the institutional atmosphere of a hospital. Yet relatively few now achieve this last ambition. The principal reason for this would seem to be not that the necessary drugs to ease the difficulties of the last days are not suitable for use at home, but that the provision of people to administer them and provide round-the-clock care is lacking.

Families, unfamiliar with the problems of nursing the dying, need help and support, and relief from the demands of twenty-four hours a day nursing. 'Heavy nursing' can be done by the community nurse but this still leaves the need for more routine care. At present, the NHS makes no provision to fill this gap and the social services find it difficult to meet their obligations to provide a night sitting service.

Dr J. W. Baker, a general practitioner in Kent, working from the Woodlands Health Centre in Tonbridge, has established a scheme of voluntary helpers to try to meet this need in local villages. The group, which calls itself Care Unlimited, consists of about sixteen people, eight of whom form the hard core, while the rest are sometimes available. Dr Baker describes their duties and the organisation of the group (Baker, 1978a):

Since the heavy nursing is done by the District Nurses, their job is to sit with the patient, to move him or her in bed as needed, to supply medicine and drinks as needed, and in general to tend. I could as well use the word nurse, but this word has implications with regard to training which prohibits its use. We are relying on the sensitivity, the common sense, and the ability to learn of well balanced people. They have had some instruction, and we, the doctors, nurses and the Group, are learning how to talk and what to say to people who are dying and their relatives, as we go along.

All the members of the group are on the telephone. If a doctor comes across a problem he rings the secretary of the groups, who then rings round the rest. Usually within a couple of hours, she rings back to say that there is someone or two people to go in for that particular night or nights. They have had some financial support from Social Services, to the tune of £150. Expenses are small but are there. The attendants are not paid.

Dr Baker is convinced that if money could be found more help would be forthcoming: 'There is an enormous reservoir of untrained but skilful people in the community who can do this work . . . The failure of this society', he comments, 'is that when it sees a need it thinks immediately in terms of bricks and mortar, and not of people . . . [but] nearly everyone has a bed in his/her own home and that is the proper place to die' (Baker, 1978b).

(2)   *The Hospital*

An experiment in democratic ward management. Hospitals are well known as examples of elaborate hierarchical structures, strict adherence to rules, and formal relations between different grades of staff and between staff and patients. These arrangements are typically justified in terms of the need to ensure scrupulously high standards of care and, in the case of relationships between ward staff and patients, to protect the former from the strains and anxieties of dealing with the sick, and sometimes dying, patient. But from a participative perspective a highly formalised regime of this kind appears as invalid in a hospital as in any other organisation, a recipe for the alienation of both staff and patient. An opportunity to test out the viability of a more participative approach to ward management was presented to a young ward sister in a London teaching hospital in the late 1960s. Shirley Kean had just been promoted from staff nurse to take charge of a neurological/neurosurgical ward. A course she had recently attended on nursing management had encouraged the adoption of more participative methods. She decided to try to apply them systematically in her new post and to keep a detailed record of what happened. She was helped by a series of fortunate circumstances including changes in higher management, the geographical remoteness of her ward from the main hospital and the appointment of two new staff nurses who were ready and willing to co-operate. This account of the fortunes of her experiment is drawn from a long paper which she wrote after she had left the hospital, 'Towards democratic ward management'.

The ward had twenty-two beds and a nursing staff of fourteen: a ward sister, three staff nurses, and a changing rota of ten student nurses who stayed between eight and ten weeks on the ward. At the beginning of the experiment it was managed in a conventional way with clear-cut hierarchy of authority, division of labour and insistence on strict adherence to detailed rules and regulations. Students had little say in daily ward administration and patients none. Relations between senior and junior staff were strictly formal and impersonal.

The aims of the experiment, which were fully discussed with the staff nurses, and approved by them were (Kean, 1972, pp. 6–7):

> to adopt a more 'patient-centred' approach to ward adminis-
> tration, which would mean involving both the patients and
> the student nurses much more in the day-to-day organisation
> of work. Since student nurses often had more 'bed-side' contact
> with patients than did the senior staff, it was felt that they often
> knew more about patients' needs and feelings; moreover, the fact
> that they were 'merely' student nurses did not mean that their
> thoughts and ideas were not equally as valuable as those of their
> senior counterparts. Above all, given that any ward/hospital
> exists for the curing of patients, the feelings of the latter group
> must be heard and given first consideration as far as is humanly
> possible. It was also hoped that this would lead to better
> relationships between all members of nursing staff and patients,
> and to an increase in work satisfaction, thus all leading ultimately
> to better patient care.
>
> In short, it was necessary to promote the sharing of power,
> knowledge, feelings and ideas.

The changes proposed were (1) that student nurses could attend all ward meetings and ward rounds, provided adequate and continuous patient care could be assured, (2) they could discuss progress reports made on them, and submit their own reports, (3) Christian names could be used freely, (4) at shift changeovers the old system of staff nurse reporting and handing over to staff nurse would be replaced by shifts handing over to each other and the incoming shift planning its work together, (5) there would be weekly meetings of all nursing staff, and of nursing staff and all patients.

When these plans were discussed with student nurses their response was 'guarded, bewildered and rather negative', but this in no way weakened the resolve of the ward sister and her colleagues to go ahead. In its first weeks, Shirley Kean reports, the new system created a high level of anxiety amongst the majority of student nurses and considerable mistrust of her personally. As time went on she noted more reassuring developments. The large majority of student nurses showed increased self-confidence, greater ability to take and enjoy responsibility, greater initiative, and were less submissive and more questioning towards their superiors. Particular gains were demonstrated in nurses' increased willingness and ability to work on their own, and to cope in emergency situations.

Most nurses seemed to obtain greater work satisfaction. Although nurses became more aware of the difficulties facing management there was more optimism that changes could be made. 'Nurses worked harder, would stay longer, volunteer to do things connected with the ward in their off duty, and asked to remain on the ward for longer than their prescribed period, or to return later in their training' (Kean, 1972, p. 12).

The pattern of work and personal relations changed in the nursing group. There was less division of labour, more sharing of tasks, reporting and observations were improved as there was less duplication of effort, communication between different levels in the nursing hierarchy was much freer and relations between nurses became more warm and caring as they got to know each other better. Feelings were more freely and openly expressed.

Relationships with patients were also affected. The usual professional barrier between the two was more frequently broken down, and heightened emotional difficulties could result. However, Shirley Kean says it was her impression that although initially this made the situation more stressful for the nurse, 'because there were opportunities for discussing these problems, the overall result was a *lowering* of anxiety and stress. The large majority expressed relief at being able to talk about such matters . . .' (p. 14).

On their side, the increased openness of expression also appeared to affect patients. They seemed more able to talk about the things which distressed them most. Although ties with nurses became closer this did not seem to increase the patients' dependency. Indeed,

quite the reverse effect was observed as they exhibited an increased
desire to help themselves (p. 21):

> they repeatedly expressed feelings of 'safety' and 'want to risk
> having another go'. Interestingly, they did not seem to develop
> more intense attachment to individual nurses but what did
> develop was a strong sense of belonging to a close-knit 'family'
> and identification with it . . . A reciprocity of help and concern
> developed between nurses and patients and between patients
> themselves. Thus patients would help each other bath, dress,
> wash, etc., and many were the late night discussions about family
> problems. The help given to the nurses (making beds, cleaning
> lockers, making drinks, etc.) was in quantity and quality, well
> above the usual standard.

The immediate effect on relatives was to make them feel rejected,
excluded from the cosy ward family. The nurses responded,
however, by encouraging them to talk more to them and the medical
staff and to feed, wash and actively help in the recovery of the
patient. Most responded positively to these opportunities (p. 22):

> They felt 'less in the dark' and better able to understand what the
> patient's illness and period of hospitalisation meant to him. Also
> they were more able to talk about what it meant for the family as
> a whole. In terms of the future they felt better supported and less
> isolated.

There is no space to discuss the impact of the experiment on other
groups of staff, nor the difficulties experienced by a small minority of
nurses. Enough evidence has been presented to show why the
originators of the scheme, at least, were convinced that their sixteen-
month experiment had demonstrated the advantage of more
participative forms of management in one of the innermost bastions
of traditional organisation.

Foster grandparents for children in hospital. A smaller-scale but
none the less significant attempt to break down the institutionalising
features of the hospital regime is represented by the foster
grandparents scheme. The adverse effects hospitals can have on
young children has long been recognised and many hospitals now
encourage one or other of the parents to come in with their child.

But what happens when the family cannot arrange to do this? The foster grandparent scheme was devised to meet just such a situation. As one of us has noted elsewhere (Hadley and Scott, 1980, pp. 92–3):

> The scheme aims to recruit people who can spend a substantial amount of time with the child each day, and sometimes stay right round the clock if the child is very ill or disturbed. Where foster grannies have been recruited, as in the Brook and Kings College Hospitals in London, they have often proved very successful. Not only have the children found a friend in the alien environment of the hospital, but the foster grandparent, who may see little of her own grandchildren, can get great satisfaction from the relationship as well.

The main difficulty experienced so far seems to have been in recruiting enough foster grandparents. This is partly because of the demanding nature of the work but also partly because some hospital staff have made little effort to welcome the foster grandparents or keep them informed about the development of the child's treatment.

The hospital at home. A development of potentially far-reaching importance in recent years has been the attempt to provide home treatment for some categories of patients who would normally have been admitted to hospital. So far there have been few moves in this direction in Britain although a DHSS-sponsored project has begun to try out a scheme in Peterborough. Nevertheless, the significance of the hospital-at-home approach in terms of developing collaboration between the formal statutory services and the informal carers is such that it seems worth including a brief description of French experience where practice is much further advanced. These notes are based on the report of Freda Clarke, a British social worker who observed the scheme in action in Paris in the mid-1970s.

The hospital at home was introduced in Paris in 1961 and was based on schemes developed in New York and Quebec. Within ten years it had expanded until it provided the equivalent service to a 900-bed hospital at one-third of the cost (Clarke, 1974, p. 387):

> The service operates through small multi-disciplinary teams each based at a hospital and serving a geographically defined area. These consist of a social worker, a nursing supervisor, ten nurses,

eight nursing aids and home helps. Each team covers 50 to 80
patients. The scheme covers all age groups and meets the needs of
a wide variety of conditions, medical and surgical, including
amputations, fractures, strokes, cancer, heart and respiratory
diseases. It has proved particularly valuable in the care of children
and the elderly and has reduced the duration of ordinary hospital
admissions. The service is deeply appreciated by the patient and
his family.

The scheme is based on the view that the home environment can
be an important factor in recovery. At the time of the study, patients
were first admitted to hospital for assessment, but the institutional
period was kept to a minimum. Criteria for participation in the
service are strict, as are arrangements to prevent hospitals using it as
a means of getting rid of unwanted patients. The patient, relatives,
general practitioner and hospital consultant must all agree, and the
doctors be willing to play their part in terms of a stipulated number
of home visits. The number of nursing hours and home help hours
required each day must not exceed a defined maximum.

Total patient care is provided – drugs, transport, X-rays, drips,
laundry, diets, physiotherapy, and so on. Given the central
importance of ensuring proper social support and the need to be able
to make a comprehensive assessment of the patient's situation, the
power to decide who shall be admitted to the scheme has been
allocated to the social worker on the team.

Psychiatric crisis intervention. Although the hospital at home is still
in its infancy in Britain something of its philosophy is
represented in the development of crisis intervention in the
treatment of the mentally ill. Psychiatric crisis intervention consists
of a team available on a twenty-four hours a day basis to make home
visits to patients or potential patients experiencing a crisis which
would normally result in immediate hospital admission. The team
aims to deal then and there with the crisis and its precipitating
conditions and to put in any help it can to stabilise the situation. In
most cases rapid intervention and intensive support enable it to
avoid admitting the patient to hospital.

Perhaps the best-known example in Britain of this approach to
psychiatric treatment is the Crisis Intervention Team at Napsbury
Hospital in Hertfordshire. The team has been operating since the
early 1970s. Its work has recently been evaluated by Dr Lawrence

Ratna, one of the psychiatrists involved (Ratna, n.d.). His study compared the outcome of crisis intervention in the Barnet area with the results of traditional community care methods used in the neighbouring area of Edgware where population size and characteristics were very similar.

The team operating the crisis intervention service at the time of the comparison (1973–5) consisted of two consultants, one medical assistant, one senior registrar, two registrars, two community nurses and three social workers. The whole team was potentially available during office hours and outside office hours two psychiatrists and one senior social worker were always on call. The team could be at the patient's home within two hours of the referral.

The crisis interview involves both assessment and treatment. 'The assessment side of the interview breaks down into two main components, namely that of clinical diagnosis in terms of symptomatology presented by the patients and secondly, an exploration of the life events which precipitated the crisis' (Ratna, n.d., p. 12). In the study period, while a majority of those diagnosed as demented or schizophrenic were offered admission at this stage, few or none of the other categories of patient were admitted.

Follow-up has been found to differ according to the problem diagnosed. Most of the diagnostic groupings were dealt with at out-patient clinics by a doctor and/or social worker. But personality disorders were followed up in patients' own homes over a long period by community nurses. Ratna comments (p. 14) that

> This policy of taking treatment to the personality disorder and of maintaining a constant relationship over a long period, rather than expecting the patient to come up regularly to an outpatient clinic is probably a factor which enables the crisis service to defuse those crises that personality disorders generate from time to time, without having to resort to admission.

The second part of the assessment is to look for the possibility of underlying life problems. Psycho-social conditions such as separation from a parent or child, spouse or lover, death, old age and disability were associated with more than half the cases referred. Where such factors were assessed as a significant factor in the illness, admission to hospital was rare and intensive social and family intervention was adopted instead.

Shifting the focus of treatment from the hospital to the family and

the community has had a dramatic effect on hospital admissions and
length of stay, as the comparison study showed. The Barnet team
admitted 43 per cent fewer patients than the community care team in
Edgware. Further, it had less than half the number of long-stay
patients of the Edgware team (Ratna, p. 7):

The ability of the crisis service to discharge the institutionally
dependent chronic patient may be related to the fact that it is able
to provide more effective support to the family in comparison to a
community care programme which tends to rely mainly on day
hospitals, hostels, out-patients clinics and the administration of
depot drugs by community nurses.

The financial saving to the NHS of the crisis intervention method
would appear to be substantial. The Barnet team, for example, is
able to serve a population of 156,000 with a single admission ward
of twenty-six beds. 'This works out to 0·2 bed/1,000 population,
well below the DHSS minimum of 0·5/1,000. Taking the cost of
maintaining an admission bed as £150 per week, this represents a
saving of nearly half a million pounds per year in one sector of the
hospital alone' (Ratna, n.d., p. 28). This is not the least of the
advantages of the scheme for, as Ratna points out, it offers the
opportunity to a whole range of paramedical personnel such as
social workers, psychologists and lay workers to form an integral
part of the team and enlarge the role they play. 'The catholicity and
flexibility of crisis theory permits the creative synthesis of theories
and therapists.' Most significant is the potential of this method for
contributing to the prevention of mental disorders. 'The experience
generated by the observation and treatment of crises has and will
generate knowledge concerning their adaptive resolution. The
knowledge would be the basis for the planning and provision of
preventive services' (Ratna, n.d., p. 29).

Education

The field of primary and secondary statutory education is one in
which the professionals have most vigorously defended their
autonomy in resisting both the influence of the educational
bureaucracies above them and the pressures from 'below' of parents
and students. 'Teaching is for experts', the argument goes, 'and we

must be left with a free hand if we are to do our job properly.' Within each institution, however, although the teacher may be the undisputed master of his classroom, a hierarchy of command exists and the head is the absolute ruler of the school. Neither parents nor pupils have any significant role in the running of the school.

Of course, not all state schools correspond exactly to this somewhat extreme characterisation but relatively few are organised in ways which suggest the pursuit of opposing values. In this section we describe one of the few exceptions, Countesthorpe College in Leicestershire.

Countesthorpe College

Countesthorpe College was opened in 1970 as an upper school for 1,400 boys and girls between 14 and 18 and a community college. The design of the building, with large open-plan carpeted spaces, as well as some conventional classrooms, signalled the intention to develop new teaching methods. The first head of the college, Tim McMullen, soon made it clear that he hoped the college would depart in other ways from traditional schools. He intended that it should be run by the staff as a whole, not himself as the head. He would take part in discussions on the management of the school but would carry out the decisions reached, even if he personally was not in agreement with them. He also hoped that students and parents would come to participate in the process of management.

A general assembly or moot was established to take all major policy decisions. Teachers and non-teaching staff were members, and eventually any parents and older students who wanted to could also attend and take part. The moot turned out to be too unwieldy for day-to-day decisions and it was decided to divide the staff into four rotating standing committees to run the school. But the moot could still be called if anyone wanted to challenge the decisions of these committees.

From the start teaching was based on individual work with children and the aim of building courses for each pupil related to their interests and capacities. In the early years it became apparent that the system was not working well, at least for the younger students. Virginia Makins, correspondent of the *Times Educational Supplement*, commented (1977, p. 35):

Part of the trouble was undoubtedly that the teachers had been over-ambitious and over-optimistic about how much they could lay on in terms of fairly individualised curriculum options, in a brand new school which was innovating on all fronts. The school's reprographic machinery purred away producing endless worksheets – but their quality was variable, and even when they were good, it rapidly became clear that a worksheet-based curriculum was a pretty dreary affair. There was no time for proper planning of courses, the resources were poorly co-ordinated, and one suspects for the non-exam students the menu ended up like a poor Chinese restaurant – apparent variety, but everything tasting the same.

Difficulties with the curriculum were compounded by increasing vandalism and sensational attacks in the local press. At the end of the fourth term the head resigned as a result of ill-health. But his resignation was not the signal for a general retreat to more traditional methods. The new head, John Watt, made it clear that he shared the goals of his predecessor and was not worried by the prospect of public criticism (Makins, 1977, p. 37):

If our objective is to assist the students to take increasing control of their own destinies, to question assumptions, to solve problems by being inventive and trained to envisage speculative alternatives, we are bound to meet conflict within an industrial society that sees schools principally as the sorting house for employment.

After considerable discussion the school decided to tackle its difficulties in finding an appropriate structure for its goal of pupil-centred learning by going over to team teaching, or 'schools within the school'. It was felt that the original attempt to combine individual autonomy with a common core curriculum – maths, sciences, humanities and arts – had failed because teachers had not been sufficiently close to the students to understand their particular needs and potentials (Armstrong and King, 1977, p. 54):

We began to see that the context we needed in order to make a success of student autonomy was one in which teachers and students could take part in a kind of continual conversation with each other – not a dialogue, discussion, or argument but something more free-ranging, intimate, expressive and egalitarian, that is to say, a conversation. Only through conversation, so we felt, could a teacher learn to identify and value the intellectual demands and interests of his students and a student those of his teacher.

The teams established consist of between 100 and 150 students and five to eight staff. The staff usually include specialists from maths, English and social studies. They have responsibility for both academic and pastoral aspects of the students' lives. The team operates from its own area or set of rooms. The students' time is divided into two halves. One half is spent with the team, the other with specialist teachers from outside the team. Individual timetables are worked out with each student and there is no streaming or setting. The difference between team teaching and teaching by outside specialists is more a matter of relationships between the student and staff than the academic content of their work. In the team (Armstrong and King, 1977. p. 56):

> the relationship between teacher and student is intended to be as many-sided as possible. The team's overriding objective is to help its students to make sense of autonomy and to put it to use in the expansion of intellect and personality . . . Sometimes [the teacher] . . . will be teaching his own individual specialism, sometimes following the particular interests and concerns of the student, sometimes teacher and student will be working together on activities neither is necessarily familiar with. The teacher has to be ready with his own ideas and responsive to those of his students over a very broad area of knowledge. The boundaries between 'academic' and 'pastoral', between teacher and taught, become, of necessity, elusive and shifting within the team situation.

Virginia Makins assessed progress three years after the team system had been introduced and on the whole was very impressed. In spite of the early criticisms of some parents and others outside the school, formal exam results differed little from other schools with similar intakes. But exam work alone is hardly a fair test of a school with aims such as Countesthorpe and Virginia Makins comments (1977, p. 46):

> What is exceptional at Countesthorpe is the freedom students have to concentrate on one project, or to take a far greater range of work than a normal timetable will allow. A few bright students

are getting through an enormous amount, with the guidance of both their tutors and specialist staff. Some students who could in no conventional terms be called bright are doing impressive work in one field that interests them. At the other end of the scale, students who came in at 14 hostile to any idea of school work have been lured back by first being allowed to do very little, then to concentrate on one thing that catches their interest.

An inspection of the school by the Department of Education as early as 1973 noted the exceptional warmth and trust between staff and students. Two years later, Virginia Makins made the same point even more forcibly. Having commented positively on the effective system of staff participation in the school, she said (p. 50):

If the democracy is a success, the staff–student relations are a triumph. It is impossible to spend five minutes in the school without seeing examples of the 'exceptional warmth and trust' noted by HM inspectors. The belief that, at least for older students in compulsory education, old-style sanctions simply do not work and, if anything, exacerbate difficulties, and the determination to work by persuasion and consent, seem to have been entirely justified in practice.

The personal social services

The changes leading to the unification of the personal social services in a single local authority department in 1971 have already been discussed above, in Chapter 5. We noted there that in spite of the Seebohm Committee's intention that the new departments should develop close links with the community and bring voluntary organisations and volunteers into close collaboration, in most authorities the organisations seem more governed by professional and bureaucratic ideologies than a community orientation. Although community care policies have been endorsed by successive governments since the early 1960s, few departments have given more than token support to informal and formally organised voluntary action. Furthermore, the recruitment of volunteers to work directly with the departments has not been pursued with uniform enthusiasm and most commonly those who are enlisted are relegated to marginal or dogsbody roles (Holme and Maizels, 1978).

Residential care, in spite of the mounting evidence against it, is still used widely for children and adolescents. And homes for the elderly, in spite of the searching criticism of Townsend and his colleagues nearly two decades ago, continue in far too many cases to be run on hierarchical lines, with minimal involvement of clients and the surrounding community.

Nevertheless, in several social services departments promising initiatives have been taken in recent years to establish more community-oriented policies. We have space to refer to no more than a small sample of these. Our focus is on (1) examples of attempts to involve the public more actively in the care of particular client groups; (2) client involvement in residential care; (3) experiments in the reorganisation of area teams so that they are better placed to develop preventive, community-oriented strategies.

Lay involvement in statutory community care services

Two examples are briefly described here of methods being developed to use the resources of ordinary citizens in providing care in the community for particular client groups: adolescents and the elderly and mentally handicapped. A third development discussed is that of paid good neighbours.

Fostering difficult adolescents. While the fostering of young children has been common practice for a long time, it has always been much more difficult to find foster homes for teenage children and particularly for the badly disturbed amongst them. In 1975 the SSD in Kent launched a scheme to recruit foster parents for disturbed adolescent children in their care. Any child in the difficult-to-foster age-range of 14–17 would be eligible for the scheme, and the foster parents were offered a decent wage for the job and given active support by the department. In 1978, for example, foster parents were offered £41 a week in addition to £18 for board, whereas the normal payment for a 15-year-old foster child would have totalled no more than £18. The first group of foster parents was given briefing lectures and seminars by the department. Subsequently they formed a group of their own to give each other support and provide an opportunity to discuss particular problems. The scheme involves a three-way written contract between the foster parents, the children and the department. This spells out the part each is expected to play, how long the initial period of foster care will be and the consequence of any party breaking the contract (Shaw, 1978).

As time has gone on the foster parents appear to have taken an increasingly central part in running the scheme. A recent account of the scheme quoted the example of one foster parent as typical (Shaw, 1978):

This foster parent seems to make many of the important decisions on the 'treatment' of the children. She says she used to ring the social worker the minute anything went wrong, but now feels that it is her responsibility. 'After all, what can they do? They are only people, like me, and I know my foster children best.'

The same account described the increasing role of the foster parents' group in selecting new foster parents and the challenge this has posed for professional social workers who previously carried the major responsibility for the care of children of the kind involved in the scheme. A senior worker commented:

I was one of those whose job it was to assess foster parents. This was seen as a very skilled operation. Now they seem to select each other.

Under the special placement scheme anyone intending to undertake the fostering of difficult children must attend group meetings of the established foster parents who play a large part in deciding whether or not they are suitable candidates for the job – although the final decision must rest with the project social officer and the division. It has been difficult to accept the power of these groups – a smack in the eye to find mainly untrained people doing the job I was trained to do.

This worker still had some misgivings about the demands that were being made on foster parents but was enthusiastic in her support for the project as a whole, and was clear that it was succeeding better than traditional methods.

The project organiser, Nancy Hazel, reported that the scheme seemed to be working well for the adolescents, their families of origin and the fostering families (Hazel, 1978, pp. 100–1):

The project placements appear to work for delinquents, in that so far many of them appear to settle happily into family life, do well at work and school and appear to lose interest in delinquent activities. Emotionally disturbed, backward or institutionalised adolescents also do well. Except for a few brief sorties, no-one has run away. The families of origin appear to like family placements, and contact by the boys and girls with their own homes usually leads either to an improvement in family relationships or to the adolescent's choosing the independence of a young adult.

The foster families report high job satisfaction and in the first two years of the scheme only one family dropped out. The reasons for this job satisfaction seem to have something to do with the current changes in family roles. The wives, who have usually worked until the arrival of the first child, no longer see themselves as fully occupied in the long run by the tasks of child care and home making. Many women need the social and intellectual rewards of work more than the financial gain – although this is very important and families with a mortgage to pay off may plan this in the expectation of two incomes.

It seems that the project offers a career which is attractive to intelligent married women who welcome the challenge of a difficult task and the intellectual challenge of defining and evaluating their work.

The first independent evaluation, undertaken after two years, suggested there was solid evidence to support these views. A study by Margaret Yelloly found that 70 per cent of the children had improved and that 64 per cent had completed their stay as set out in the contract. Partly as a result of the scheme the department was able to reduce the proportion of children in care in residential homes from 47 per cent in 1975 to 37 per cent at the beginning of 1978 (Shaw, 1978).

Community care for the elderly. Kent is also developing a scheme of paid good neighbours to help postpone or prevent the need for residential care for the elderly. Up to two-thirds of the cost of a place in a residential home can be spent by community support services for a group of frail and isolated elderly people who might otherwise have to be admitted to residential care. In addition to standard services such as those of the home help, good neighbours are paid to visit and help care for the old people, perhaps doing shopping and cooking for them, as well as taking them out and helping to reduce their isolation and loneliness in other ways. Pay averages £5 to £6 (1979) a week. It is reported that payment increases the element of consistency in the support given to the elderly. It also enables people to undertake the work who could not otherwise afford to do it. The scheme appears to attract a significant proportion of working-class good neighbours, as the Kent project leader remarks: 'We have avoided the stereotype of middle-class ladies with time on their hands, and instead we are tapping a different source of volunteers. A large number of them are working class, and they have a wide variety of backgrounds' (Whitehouse, 1978).

Objections that paid volunteer schemes are likely to kill off unpaid voluntary work have not been borne out by the Kent scheme. The social services' research officer claims that 'The availability of payment is stimulating community volunteering rather than replacing it, and all the evidence so far shows that the project is a catalyst, not a killer, of neighbourly goodwill' (ibid.).

The scheme is being evaluated by researchers at the University of Kent. They are comparing elderly clients allocated to the project with a control group who receive the normal range of services provided by the SSD. The evaluation of the first seventy cases studied – thirty-five in the experimental group and thirty-five in the control group – suggests the value of the scheme (Challis and Davies, 1980). After one year a third (twelve) of the control group had been admitted to old people's homes compared with a ninth (four) of the experimental group. Furthermore, independent assessment of the old people in both groups suggested that the condition of several of those in the experimental group had actually improved over the year in a number of important ways. They were considered to need less help in the home, to be less socially isolated, to be less lonely and to have higher morale. These improvements were achieved at a significantly lower overall cost to the SSD than the services provided to the old people in the control group.

Another example in which 'paid volunteers' are used in the care of the elderly is the Liverpool Good Neighbour Scheme. This is not organised by the social services department but is run by Age Concern with funds provided by the department. At present three districts of the city are covered by the scheme. In 1978 the total cost was £50,000. Each district is run by a paid organiser who has part-time clerical assistance. Funds are sufficient to recruit fifty good neighbours in each area. The good neighbours are paid £4·50 a week plus 50p travel in return for a minimum of fifteen hours' work (1978 rates). Far more people have applied for the work than can be taken on and a careful selection procedure is used when appointments are made. The duties undertaken by the good neighbours include all kinds of practical help, with the exception of such household tasks as are considered to be the job of the home help. The good neighbours make weekly reports to the organiser when they collect their wages, and these occasions provide a valuable opportunity for them to seek advice and support in their work. Age Concern comments that payment is important in 'reinforcing the feeling in the Good Neighbours that their work has to be done at the right time and in a proper manner'. It is also claimed that it has enabled the organiser to make demands on the good neighbours that could not readily be made of volunteers. But the organisation is at pains to point out that this is not a normal employer–employee relationship. Almost all good neighbours spend considerably more time on their work than the fifteen hours a week they have agreed to take on. Further, payment has not hindered in any way the development of close relationships between good neighbour and client (Age Concern Training Department, 1978).

Many elderly people have become firmly established as friends of the families of the good neighbours. The frequency with which such relationships occur suggests that paid good neighbours do not regard their work as merely a chore with cash as the main basis for their commitment.

Schemes involving paid neighbourly help have become increasingly widespread in recent years, although there is remarkably little systematic evidence available about them. A review of the home help service in the early 1970s estimated that at that time there were between fifty and sixty schemes in England. Rates of pay were at or rather below those for home helps (DHSS, 1973, pp. 30, 34).

Self-help in residential and day care

Residential care of the elderly offers perhaps the most extreme example of the passive role expected of the social services client. Material standards in many old people's homes are often excellent today, a far cry from the ex-workhouse establishments that Peter Townsend described two decades ago in *The Last Refuge* (1964). But inside the new purpose-built homes the regime is all too likely to be unchanged, and the roles of staff and residents as far apart as ever. The staff usually see it as their job to manage the institution and expect the residents to accept the routines and rules they establish. Whether it is intended or not, the end product of the system as far as most residents are concerned is passivity and inactivity. On any day of the week, unless they are having their meals or there is a break for bingo or some other entertainment, the old people will be found sitting in lines of easy chairs, staring out of the window, or watching television, or simply waiting for some small event to disturb the tedium of their lives. Their submission to such an existence is hardly surprising for the earlier phases of old age have been an apprenticeship in resignation and withdrawal. *Guardian* writer Helen Franks comments (1979):

> We make our ageing population lose earning power and status; we make them redundant and useless. And then, having devalued them we isolate and ignore them so that by the time they are really old they have become cowed, helpless, a generation of depressed drop-outs.
>
> It is no wonder that they don't make friends with each other – they have been dumped together, a constant reminder of their impotence. It is no wonder they turn lazy, self-centred, ungrateful. It is difficult to remain outward-looking, positive, if everything you have been used to doing for yourself is done for you.

But the story does not have to end in this way. There are now a number of homes where the residents are actively encouraged to take a part in the management, and to do as many things for themselves as they can. One example, Dawes House in Wandsworth, was recently described by Helen Franks. The home was built in 1975 by the local authority. Residents have their own bed-sitting rooms which they can keep as they like. They are encouraged to clean their own rooms, make their beds, do their own hand washing. They help out the staff with office chores, take on responsibility for welcoming new residents, have their own kitchenettes in which they can make themselves hot drinks and snacks. Residents have a committee which arranges their entertainment and they have come to take a lively interest in health matters too. Few drugs are given in the home and there is virtually no sedation. The local GP comes in to eat his breakfast with the residents and as a result of his influence they have decided to switch to wholemeal bread and bran cereals after 'a lifetime's allegiance to white sliced'.

This new approach to residential care was carefully planned. The home (Franks, 1979) chose its staff as well as its residents carefully. The former were given special training, taught how not to interfere or let routine take over; the latter knew the philosophy in advance and were prepared to look after themselves and not see the demands made upon them as a sign of neglect or an imposition. They had, of course, to be relatively fit and mobile.

Some may suggest that this last condition, the requirement that the residents must be reasonably fit, will automatically rule out the introduction of such regimes as that established at Dawes from many homes where the large majority of the residents are very frail. But this may well be a question of the *proportions* of residents in different states of health. Clearly, if all or nearly all are so frail or confused that they cannot care for themselves the system will not work. But if there is a more balanced mix of the fit and the less fit it may function well. The experience of Dawes is relevant here. Helen Franks got to know the home four years after it had been established:

> In four years old people can age a great deal, and at Dawes their selected group is growing frailer and more infirm. They are aware that there comes a time to leave a person in peace, to let him or her withdraw from the present and rely on the care and protection of others. There are those who no longer clean their rooms or have their jobs of laying or clearing the tables in the dining rooms. They may choose without pressure to stay in bed till midday or have their meals in their rooms. To some who are becoming confused, a blind eye is turned to hand washing left forgotten all day in the washbasin. It is encouraging that they are still doing it at all. And it is encouraging that the Dawes House philosophy seems to be surviving the test.

Dawes is not unique. For example, in Wiltshire where the director of social services has spent much of his working life in the field of residential care, two homes have been opened which are run on very similar lines and apparently with the same kind of results. Indeed, in recent years an increasing number of local authorities have designed their new old people's homes so that the residents are split into small groups and can more readily take a share in managing their own lives in the institutions. As at Dawes, however, the attitude and commitment of staff appears to be crucial. A survey of the design of sixty-seven old people's homes, some of them still under construction, showed that forty were planned for group living (Wyvern Partnership . . ., 1979). But the same study showed that of the forty-four homes on which full information was available only seven had a management regime which actively encouraged the residents to organise their own lives. Clearly the attitude and commitment of staff are crucial and the development of schemes such as those at Dawes must depend to a considerable extent on the capacity of social services departments to change the approach of existing personnel or recruit people more sympathetically disposed to the establishment of self-managing regimes.

Day centres for the handicapped and elderly often exhibit many of the same dependency-creating features as residential institutions. Typically a centre's programme is planned and managed by paid staff with little or no consultation with its users. Frequently the daily routine includes long periods of passivity when there is little to stimulate or interest those using the centre. It is little wonder if they soon become dull and apathetic.

But is there any more reason why a day centre should be run in this non-participative way than an old people's home? An experiment in Stockport in the organisation of a day centre for the physically handicapped suggests the potential for active user involvement.

The Primus Club. In 1975 a pilot study on day centres by Jan Carter and her colleagues asked why ideas of self-management had apparently not been tried amongst disabled people. The social services department at Stockport had participated in the study and decided to take up the challenge the study put forward. A new day centre for the physically handicapped was about to be opened and the assistant director of social services offered the forty handicapped people who were to use the centre the opportunity to take over its management. Initially their response was cautious and even suspicious but today, according to Jan Carter, members are enthusiastic about the experiment (Carter, 1981, ch. 18):

Most centre members are middle-aged, with acquired disabilities, such as arthritis and strokes. Most need help, or at least aids, to talk, walk, or toilet themselves. The members elect a management committee from amongst themselves annually and the committee then runs the centre. Accountable to the local authority social services committee via the assistant director of social services, the committee pays the bills and controls the budget. One member of the social services day care advisory staff also sits on the committee and the assistant director is *ex officio*.

The members decided that the basic activity at the centre should be craft work: they make crafts, sell them, the proceeds build up the amenity fund, and then, rather than paying individuals for their work each week, the group 'rewards' itself every now and then. Last week, for instance, the members had a big evening out in the restaurant of a local 'good food' hotel. The crafts done at the centre are simply handicrafts, such as crocheting and basketry, usually known already to the members themselves. They teach each other, although the local authority can make a handicraft instructress available as a consultant.

The care staff employed to work in the centre are accountable to the user management committee, which functions in place of a head of centre. The committee has had to learn the diplomacy of industrial relations: for instance, how to persuade the cook to provide the menu the users would like. Some committee members have experience to contribute from their past work background, but not all: the backgrounds of members are very mixed.

Discussion

These developments have grown up on a piecemeal basis, largely independent of each other. Nevertheless, certain common features can clearly be found within them in terms of the values pursued, and the structures and processes developed to implement them. Indeed, it is possible to identify the beginnings of a coherent alternative approach to the present dominant system of social services organisation.

As we have already suggested, different systems of government imply different functions for social policy and different structures to apply it. In earlier chapters we examined facets of social policy that had arisen under the *representative system* of government which currently prevails in this country. To recapitulate, the elected member is seen as the sole legitimate repository of authority and the social services (as with other instruments of government policy) are designed to carry out policies determined by him. Administrators and professionals are seen at any rate in theory as servants of the representative assembly and are expected to adhere strictly to these policies. The citizen, in his role as consumer, is assumed to have a largely passive role, and is expected to accept the services provided for him.

The developments reviewed in this chapter fit uncomfortably with this model of service delivery. Indeed, in so far as they embody a common philosophy this relates much more closely to that implied by a *participatory*, rather than a representative, model of democracy. In such a system, while the general directions of social policy are still determined by the elected members of central and local government, the ways in which the policies are developed and applied are open to discussion and amendment by both social services staff and clients, for their involvement is regarded as indispensable if available resources are to be maximised and variations in need/demand are to be recognised.

With the help of the examples of the schemes discussed in this chapter it is now possible to begin to identify some of the more salient characteristics of social services organisation implied in participatory organisations and to compare them with the features of the currently dominant system, based on bureaucratic and professional criteria derived from the representative model of democracy.

The *underlying function* of the bureaucratic social service organisation is to carry out the delivery of a predetermined service to a well-defined client group. In contrast, the participatory organisation operates with much wider terms of reference which encourage a co-operative and entrepreneurial approach. Aims are defined in collaboration with staff and users as, for example, in Countesthorpe where teachers and students define goals together, or in the democratic nursing experiment in which both nurses and patients shared in decision-making. The most is made of whatever resources are available in carrying out the aims, including volunteers, as in the cases of the care of the dying and the foster grandparent scheme, and clients, as in the old people's home and day centre for the physically handicapped.

Authority in the bureaucratic model clearly reposes in the organisational hierarchy. The only exception is where a professional has been given an area of discretion and his professional knowledge and status are the source of his right to take decisions. In the participatory model authority is only based in part on formal position and qualifications. Practical knowledge, personal commitment and position in the community are also sources of authority. We have seen examples in the fostering of adolescents, where the knowledge and experience of the foster parents soon was superior in some respects to those of the social workers, and in the care of the dying, where the untrained carers acquired special insight and understanding through their accumulated experience.

In bureaucratic social service organisation *roles* of staff tend to be clearly defined. Their relationships with users are typically meant to be detached, void of personal feeling. In most circumstances the role of the user is supposed to be passive. Patterns of behaviour in participatory organisations of the kind described in this chapter sometimes differed markedly from these prescriptions. Staff roles tended to be flexible and to blur at the edges as in the democratic ward management experiment and Countesthorpe. Personal involvement of staff with individual users was a feature of most of the schemes reviewed. And the active involvement of users, as in the patients' groups, the self-help schemes in residential and day care, the democratic ward experiment and others is an important feature of the participatory system.

Innovation within bureaucratic organisations is relatively rare since the formal authority to change structures and procedures resides at the top of the hierarchy, and most employees are likely to feel bound by their tightly defined roles. In contrast, participatory organisations tend to be much more innovative both because they have more freedom to introduce change and because the wider interaction of different grades of staff and of staff with users is likely to produce more criticism and more ideas for change. All the more democratic organisations described here showed a high propensity to innovate – the patients' groups, the self-help home and day centre, the democratic ward experiment and Countesthorpe.

In bureaucratic social service organisations *indicators of performance* tend to relate to input factors such as the investment in buildings, the number of hospital beds, the number of meals delivered. This reflects in part the upwards responsibility of staff and the need for 'objective' and 'concrete' measures to meet the needs of the political heads of the organisation. Participative social service organisations are not immune to such pressures but they are likely to give much greater weight to users' views. The aim of satisfying the customer was a high priority in most of the examples discussed here. For instance, it was a primary factor in the establishment of Care Unlimited – enabling people to die at home as they wished. It was also important in the patients' groups where the doctors were seeking to establish what health needs and priorities patients had. These and other key characteristics of the two systems are summarised in Table 9.1 below.

Table 9.1 *Characteristics of social services organisation in bureaucratic and participatory systems*

Characteristics	Bureaucratic	Participatory
Function of system	Delivery of predetermined service to clearly defined client groups	Facilitation of best feasible service in collaboration with staff, clients and the community
Main source(s) of authority	The organisation; training – expertise of individual staff	The organisation; the expertise of the team; negotiated relationships with the users/community
Organisational structure	Hierarchical, large units	Flat organisations, small units
Mode of decision-making	By individual, pressures to pass up the hierarchy	By team, pressures to push down to front line
Role of worker/staff	Clearly defined and bounded	Flexible
Organisation of ancillary, volunteer	Segregated	Integrated
Role of client/user	Expected to be passive	Encouraged to be active
Character of relationships between staff and user	Strives to be neutral, disinterested	Strives to be empathetic
Contracting work out to non-statutory agencies, volunteers, etc.	Low	High
Innovation in management of the organisation from within the agency	Rare	Frequent
Principal indicators of performance	Input indicators (e.g. buildings, hospital beds, meals delivered)	Output indicators – user satisfaction, as defined by user (e.g. staying in the community, getting treatment that 'works')

Accountability	Upwards, to chief officer and representative body	Two-way: upwards (as representative); downwards – to users and staff
Definition of professionalism	Mastery of body of knowledge; application to individual cases	Expert knowledge plus capacity to recognise/work with 'non-expert' in team,etc., to maximise effectiveness

In practice, few if any of the individual schemes examined exhibit all the characteristics listed here. It would be surprising if they did for none is located within a larger organisation structured in its turn on participatory principles. Nevertheless, the evidence of the performance of these semi-participatory organisations suggests that it is already superior to that of the non-participatory, representative system organisations. It would seem reasonable to assume that if the wider context in which the organisations operated were more sympathetic, their performance would be still more impressive. While any major changes in the framework of the social services will require substantial alterations in policy (to which we turn our attention in the next chapter), it is possible to obtain a fuller picture of the shape and operation of a more comprehensive approach in one corner of the existing social services: the development of community-oriented teams in certain social services departments.

Community-oriented social services teams

The examples of innovative practice in the personal social services which were reviewed above are mainly focused on the care of particular client groups. But the elements of a common underlying philosophy can be distinguished in all of them. All identify capacities in ordinary people to provide care, or self-care. All imply pro-active rather than reactive responses to the problems involved – a preference for prevention over treatment and for teamwork over casework. Is it possible to implant these ideas, developed in the margins of the service, closer to the heart of its operations so that they may influence all aspects of its functioning? Could, for example, the area team be organised in a way that would embody these principles?

The present prevailing model of organisation of field services in the PSS is unsympathetic to such a community-centred approach, as we have already indicated in Chapter 5. Defensive, client-centred, treatment-oriented methods predominate. Nevertheless, in the last few years a number of area social services teams up and down the country have been experimenting with more community-centred methods. Although they have adopted a variety of organisational forms, reflecting in particular different local conditions and opportunities, the outline of a shared philosophy and common practice can be discerned.

The spirit in which these teams approach their work is pragmatic and entrepreneurial rather than professional or bureaucratic. They are simply concerned with using their resources in such a way as to maximise the care provided within the community to those individuals and groups in need. Fully recognising the existing importance of informally and formally organised voluntary carers in the community, the teams accept that it is an important part of their task to strengthen and develop such voluntary action. To increase the effectiveness of their own direct intervention, in cases where the community cannot cope, the teams endeavour to identify those at risk at an earlier stage and to deploy a larger proportion of their staff in front-line positions where they can provide immediate help.

The application of a strategy of this kind requires its own distinctive methods of organisation and management. These must be designed to

(1) enable front-line staff to have detailed knowledge of the area served, including its informal caring networks, relevant local and statutory organisations and their opposite numbers in the staff of these organisations;
(2) facilitate easy access by users to the team at the local level;
(3) ensure that the team has the authority and capacity to respond rapidly at local level in providing help.

These requirements lead logically to the decentralisation of services to small areas of perhaps 5,000–10,000 population and, ideally, the establishment on such 'patches' of small integrated teams of social workers, ancillaries, home helps, wardens and volunteers. In practice, few of the community-centred teams in this country have yet been able to combine as many different workers in localised teams, but several have developed other variants of the patch approach.

The main organisational characteristics implied in such an approach are summarised in Table 9.2 below. In practice few of the

Table 9.2   *Main organisational characteristics of client-centred and community-centred area teams*

Orientation Characteristics	*Client-Centred*	*Community-Centred*
Rationale	Treatment through application of specialist knowledge to clients identified by referral to the office	Prevention and treatment through strengthening informal care, voluntary organisations and the early identification of those needing direct help
Unit of organisation	Area (pop. 25,000–50,000)	Patch (pop. 5,0000–10,000)
Point of referral	Office	Patch and office
Proportion of referrals dealt with informally	Low	High
Allocation of work	Duty officer or senior social worker	Patch leader (social worker) or patch worker (ancillary)
Role of social worker	Direct involvement with cases	Management of patch team including supervision of patch workers; direct responsibility for a limited number of cases requiring professional input
Role of ancillary	Support of social worker, service delivery	Front-line worker for all cases not requiring substantial input from professional worker; in other cases, collaborator or support-worker
Organisation of domiciliary workers, community workers and volunteers	Separate from organisation of field social work	Integral in organisation of the patches

Relationships with other local agencies	Via the hierarchy, through the area office	Direct with patch workers and patch leader
Emphasis on administrative procedures	High	Low
Levels of interaction between staff of different grades	Low	High
Management styles	Blend of professional and bureaucratic; adherence to formal roles	Entrepreneurial, participative; considerable degree of autonomy on patches; free interpretation of roles

community-centred area teams have been able to integrate all their resources at a local level in a way that tests out the full potential of patch systems. Most are operating in conditions in which only some categories of workers are patched and their freedom to vary their methods of working from standardised departmental procedures, so that they can respond to differences in local needs, is limited.

Nevertheless, even in such restricted circumstances, the patch-based teams believe they have made considerable gains from adopting a community orientation. These are defined in terms of a greatly improved knowledge of the area, an increased capacity to relate the team's work to voluntary action, the earlier identification of those in need of help, reduced admission of clients of all kinds to residential instructions and better co-operation with other local voluntary and statutory agencies. A further gain which is widely reported is an increase in work satisfaction for the staff involved. This is described in terms of replacing the somewhat anomic state of the worker in a traditional team, trying to cover a large area that he or she can know little about, with the rich and intimate knowledge that the patch worker soon acquires of his small neighbourhood; the additional resources that are obtained by working closely with voluntary care systems; the feeling of being on top of the job instead of swamped by it; and the recognition and status that is typically accorded to local workers. (It is interesting to compare the experience of patch social workers with community constables working on small local beats. Claims made for the community constable system are very similar to those made for patch-based social services, including both better crime prevention and higher job satisfaction. It would seem that the same underlying principles are involved: working locally *with* the community in defining and providing a service instead of imposing a predetermined system from a headquarters remote from the people affected.)

Systematic studies of the claims made for community-oriented social services teams have only recently been initiated and it is too early to draw general conclusions about their effectiveness, or, indeed, how far their methods are generalisable to other area teams. However, there appears to be a small but growing trend towards patch-based systems in the country as a whole. At least forty area teams are known to be operating in this way in England and Wales and more are in the process of changing to patch (Hadley and McGrath, 1980a, 1980b). To give a fuller idea of how a patch-based team can be organised in practice, when there is a considerable degree of autonomy at the area level, we describe below the structure of the team at Normanton, a town in the metropolitan district of Wakefield.

Normanton is a small mining town with a population of about 18,000. It has about the average proportions of elderly people and those in other categories, such as the physically and mentally handicapped, from whom the clientele of the social services is drawn. Until 1976 social services were organised from the neighbouring town of Pontefract. In that year, however, a new area officer was appointed and it was decided to move the team to Normanton itself. The area officer, Mike Cooper, used the occasion of the move and the build-up of a new team to introduce patch methods of working. (Cooper, M., 1981)

The town is divided into three patches, covering populations varying between 5,000 and 8,000. Each patch is headed by a patch leader, who is an experienced social worker, and has two patch workers who are officially employed as ancillaries. Each patch also has about twenty-five home helps and five or six wardens, who work mainly with the elderly. The patch workers are all women, between 30 and 60 years old. They have no formal training in social work but have been selected for their sound common sense and experience. They play a key part in the system. Most of them live in the town and they all have become closely acquainted with their patches. In contrast to conventional social services departments, in which it is usual for qualified workers to filter all incoming referrals and then pass on the more routine to unqualified workers, in Normanton the patch workers occupy the front-line position. They deal directly with many of the problems referred to the team and only the cases that pose problems they cannot cope with unaided, or that departmental rules insist must be allocated to qualified workers, are passed to the patch leaders. The patch workers are widely known on their patches and pick up many of their referrals informally in the course of their daily rounds. Their work is a mixture of practical help, including the physical care of the infirm, shopping, cooking meals, counselling and advocacy. They are closely supported by their patch leaders and can turn to them for advice whenever they run into problems with which they feel unable to cope.

The patch leaders have overall responsibility for the management of the patch as well as their own caseloads, which include all statutory work with children. To allow for an element of specialisation in their caseloads, some cases are allocated across patch boundaries. The patch leaders are expected to keep an oversight of the work of the home helps and wardens in their localities, and also promote the development of community projects such as youth clubs and lunch clubs for the elderly.

Each patch has its own room in the area office and works together as a team. There is a frequent informal consultation between workers and, where it is seen as advantageous, cases are shared between patch workers, or between patch workers and the patch leader. These arrangements have the dual advantage that there is a constant source of mutual support in dealing with difficult cases and that cover is readily available for a particular case if the worker primarily responsible for it is away on another job, or is sick or on leave.

The patch workers act as the main link to the home helps and wardens in the team. Often they will be working on the same case and will meet to discuss it. But they also exchange information about others who may need help in the future. Currently, to increase this preventive aspect of the warden's job, it has been decided to reorganise their work. Instead of the present arrangement by which the wardens have responsibility for a fixed list of clients whom they must visit each day, they will be given a more general responsibility for a mini-patch, covering perhaps a population of a thousand people. They will decide themselves, in consultation with patch staff, which of the elderly require what frequency of visiting, and will devote more of their time to building up a wider range of contacts in their patch with both potential clients and potential helpers. In this way the patch teams hope they will become even more closely related to the areas they are serving.

Both the team as a whole and the individual patch teams are run on a participative basis. All the area team staff meet every week to discuss management matters and there are frequent meetings of the individual patches. From time to time the home helps and wardens also meet on a patch basis.

The area officer believes that the patch system at Normanton has led to a reduction in crisis referrals, has increased the capacity of the community to care for its own and substantially increased the amount of work undertaken by the team. He is convinced that the example of his patch workers shows that the potential of the untrained ancillary is grossly under-used in conventionally run teams. The sense of commitment and high morale which characterise his team are, he suggests, directly related to the enlargement of jobs to match people's abilities and their involvement in a co-operative venture.

The Normanton team illustrates the scope for experiment that sometimes exists within the present system but it must also be a reminder of the precariousness of such innovations. In so far as the team is deviating from standard practice within the local authority department, its developments require frequent explanation and constant defence. Much necessarily depends on the political skills and commitment of the area officer. If he moves elsewhere the future of the system may well be in jeopardy. This point has a much wider applicability than to patch systems alone. Almost all the innovative developments described in this chapter have depended upon unusual entrepreneurial skills and the conjunction of other circumstances favourable to experiment. All in some ways stand against the prevailing system and are in danger of being reincorporated in it if the impetus for change within the schemes slackens. In the long run the growth of more participatory, community-oriented organisations in the social services must depend upon sympathetic changes in the wider social institutions of which they are a part. We turn to consider the issues involved in achieving such changes in the next chapter.

CHAPTER 10

Towards Alternative Structures

The previous chapter gave practical examples of two related strategies – decentralisation and pluralism. Both were ways of widening involvement in the social services and reducing the barriers between service-givers and service-receivers. But many of the illustrations, it could well be argued, owed their existence to a few inspired individuals or could only exist in specially protected nature reserves. The question we consider in this chapter, therefore, is how to move from a few progressive experiments to more widespread change. On the conventional model of purposive social change this step is taken by means of legislation. Once government has become convinced that a new pattern is appropriate, it is imposed from above. But this is exactly the approach we have criticised. What alternative is there? Is it possible to envisage a bottom upwards rather than a top downwards form of change? In seeking to answer these questions this chapter does not adumbrate an alternative blueprint: rather it argues simply that different structures are possible.

The necessary role of government

It may be helpful to begin a discussion of alternative, more decentralised ways of providing social services by considering which functions must remain the responsibility of government. The present pattern is for government to act mainly by providing services directly. In addition, some services, such as until recently supplementary benefits, are provided through semi-autonomous quangos, though these tend to be no less centralised than government departments.

The main risks of a more decentralised and plural pattern of services are that there would be great variation between areas in the quantity and quality of services provided, and that these variations might be inversely related to need. There would, too, be a risk that any schemes for local, decentralised accountability might be abused or subverted. These risks constitute the main arguments against a more decentralised system and point towards the kind of framework that would be required by an alternative system. Such a framework would have to provide for the equitable redistribution of resources; it would have to ensure adequate standards of provision; and where the provision of services was devolved to organisations not directly accountable to it, government would still have a duty to police whatever alternative form of accountability was decided upon. Each of these three elements deserves some further examination.

Central government now influences the distribution of resources between individuals and families through the taxation system and through returning resources to people in the form of benefits and services. As noted in Chapter 4, the main redistributory effect is achieved by social security payments. These are already, and will have to go on being, an essential element in any national framework. As between areas, in the social as opposed to the economic field, the main instrument of redistribution is the rate support grant. This, too, is an essential element of a national framework. Under a more decentralised and diversified system one could envisage other organisations besides the existing local authorities receiving grants from various central agencies; but these, too, could be taken into account when allocating rate support grant, as already happens with grants made under the Urban Programme.

Redistributing resources would probably be easier than maintaining standards under a more decentralised and plural system. Certainly the abuses from time to time revealed in privately run residential institutions illustrate how things can go wrong without an effective system of monitoring. There is, however, a traditional method, best established in the education service, for maintaining professional surveillance over independent organisations by means of an inspectorate.

In the face of teachers' claims for professional autonomy this inspectoral function has come to be carried out with less rigour, and has taken on a more advisory character; while inspections of private residential establishments in the personal social services seem never to have been very rigorous. But in principle there seems to be little reason why greater decentralisation should not be accompanied by more stringent inspections. Such inspections would have to cover both the quality of service provided and the arrangements for local accountability discussed below. The latter would also of course be an important element in the arrangements for monitoring, particularly by offering clearer channels than at present for the expression of consumers' views.

As well as preventing abuse in a system less subject to hierarchical regulation, government would retain a developmental function: that is, it would have to have a positive as well as a negative approach to standards of service; and even when much more emphasis was placed on bottom upwards development, it would have to retain a capability for pursuing nationally determined priorities and encouraging activity in areas where spontaneous initiatives were weak. But this too could be achieved by means other than itself providing services directly. The Urban Programme is one illustration of how this can be done: its formula has been to stimulate local initiatives by means of grants to local organisations. There are too a number of national agencies such as the Countryside Commission and the Housing Corporation which have combined grant-giving with developmental functions. In so far as a national superstructure is required it should take on a character more of this kind. As at present constituted such agencies have rightly been criticised for being controlled by ministerial appointees who are not properly accountable either to Parliament or to anyone else. But the answer is not to absorb such agencies into government departments, thereby making them in theory more accountable to Parliament: rather ways should be found of including among the membership of their governing bodies people chosen by and accountable to the constituencies which the agency serves.

New models

Having looked briefly at an alternative framework, in effect at an alternative structure of constraints and incentives, it is necessary to ask how a new pattern of local services might come into existence and what form it might take. There is no facile answer to this question, since the developments advocated here are not readily compatible with many of the favoured nostrums of the right and the left, and they would certainly threaten some of the interests and practices of those who at present provide social services. In essence, what is required is a pattern of change which would place the emphasis on the voluntary, horizontal diffusion of ideas and practice. Innovations in professional practice tend to come about in this way, as of course do changes in taste and fashion. However, change in the social services is not just a matter of individuals acting separately, since it requires collective action and there are likely to be obstacles in the form of existing institutions and interests. There is, above all, the question of the availability of the necessary financial resources.

A sense of alternative possibilities is contained in a development that has spread more widely than most of the innovatory projects discussed in Chapter 9. Over a hundred refuges for battered women, each of them arising from a local initiative, have come into existence during the past decade. These have been helped by support from the centre. Thus the House of Commons Select Committee on Violence in Marriage report encouraged local authorities to provide backing for refuges; the DHSS has funded the National Women's Aid Federation and the Urban Programme has provided grants for individual refuges, while the Homeless Persons Act 1975 made it clear that local authorities had an obligation to house battered women. Here, then, is a widespread development which grew out of a national movement and was facilitated by central government.

The implication of this example is that some developments towards decentralisation and pluralism are compatible with existing structures. It is not difficult to envisage more developments along such lines, in particular through local authorities putting more reliance on voluntary organisations for a variety of services. The fact that a role is given to a voluntary organisation is, of course, not necessarily a step forward, since voluntary organisations do not always provide for consumer and community involvement. Nevertheless, a significant measure of progress is possible without new legislation and without the abolition of existing superstructures or the construction of new ones.

Such steps towards more decentralised and participatory structures do, however, usually require existing authorities to relinquish some of their power. This they are often unwilling to do. For example, the attempts to establish neighbourhood councils in urban areas in England have been largely frustrated by the resistance of the district councils. In contrast Scotland now has community councils covering almost the whole of the country. But this is as a result of local initiatives arising out of legislation and centrally inspired development activity. Thus local government reorganisation in Scotland provided for the establishment of what were designated community councils and for procedures by which this might take place, not according to a universal model but according to the wishes of the inhabitants of each locality. The resulting activity has been extensively researched and described (Masterson, 1980). In brief, what seems to have happened is the creation of institutions not unlike the parish councils found in rural areas in England, but differing from them in two important respects, in that they cover urban as well as rural areas and have no right to even the modest precept on the rates allowed in England. Although lack of finance will limit the activities and services that can be initiated by the community councils, many of them promise to act as a voice for their localities on a variety of issues and to be a source of voluntary initiatives. Here, therefore, is a case of local development arising from a strong central stimulus.

The right to initiate services

Following from the Scottish example, one can envisage, as a major part in any alternative model of change, a strategy for creating rights that gives people the power and the resources to take initiatives of their own. Examples of such rights might include the right to establish neighbourhood councils, the right to set up schools, the right to develop alternative housing schemes and the right to devise local health facilities. Of course, the citizen is technically free to engage in any one of these activities today, but for most people such rights are meaningless when they carry no resources with them. Our proposals imply that once certain conditions had been fulfilled, public funds would be made available to back these initiatives. We consider briefly how this might work out in the examples mentioned.

Parish councils already exist in rural areas in England and have the right to raise limited financial resources through the rating system. Neighbourhood councils might be set up as the urban counterpart of the parish councils. Covering populations of, say, 5,000–20,000, their establishment would depend on successfully activating a mechanism to provide evidence of adequate local support. As in Scotland, their continuation would depend upon the creation of a system for local accountability, involving an election in one form or another. Such councils would have two main functions: acting as a collective voice for the neighbourhood in dealing with local statutory organisations such as the planning department, the area social services team, local schools, the police, and so on; and initiating local facilities and services itself, such as visiting schemes for the elderly, youth clubs, or playgroups, as well as activities outside the field of the social services (see Hatch and Humble, 1980).

State support for education in schools not directly maintained by the local education authorities now takes two forms: subventions for individuals attending independent schools and the provision of most of the funds for what are defined as 'voluntary-aided schools'. The former is a small, state-funded route into the privileged private sector, while the latter is a continuing tribute to the religious commitments of the nineteenth century. What is needed is to secularise the voluntary-aided principle. Thus a sufficiently large group of parents, say, representing forty or more children, could be given the right to set up their own school and employ their own teachers. Any such voluntary school would have to meet certain minimal educational requirements, validated by inspection, and would be funded at the same per capita level as the local maintained schools. To prevent the system leading to greater inequality in educational provision it would be necessary to make it a condition of all schemes that (1) there would be no topping up of the state-provided funds with private fees, and (2) admission to the school would have to observe the same principles regarding balanced intakes as the local maintained system. In essence, the ideas being put forward here are similar to those canvassed by the Campaign for State Supported Alternative Schools.

In the housing field the Housing Corporation already provides the auspices under which local initiatives can be supported. In health there is no equivalent arrangement. Yet there is plenty of interest in a preventive approach to health and in alternative ways of providing health care, evidenced by the initiatives discussed in the last chapter and the growth of self-help groups. It would not be difficult to stimulate development in this field by establishing a fund to finance local initiatives. At the outset a quite modest sum would add a substantial impetus.

It is an essential feature of these initiatives that they should be permissive and not mandatory. It would be up to the people in any particular area to decide whether to take up any or all of the opportunities provided for in the schemes, whether by way of exercising rights or applying for funds. Although we see the schemes as essentially an addition to the existing provision of services, if they are successful they will necessarily begin to modify the system. For example, even if only a few groups of parents opted to open their own schools, the realisation that other parents *might* initiate them would significantly alter the balance of power within the traditional school system.

The right to participate in statutory service provision

Parallel to the development of rights to take initiatives outside statutory organisations should go the recognition of the rights of users to have a voice in the management of the statutory services themselves. However, the difficulties in prescribing a means to achieve this are considerably greater than those of designing a scheme for permissive initiatives of the kind we have just described. Public involvement in statutory services is unlikely to have much meaning or effect unless the institutions involved are themselves local and managed in an open and responsive manner. As we have seen, most statutory services are, in fact, managed on bureaucratic principles and organised in large administrative units remote from the areas they serve. General provisions for public participation, therefore, planned to cover the whole range of existing services would have little chance of success. In a sense it is already provided for through the existing local authorities, while the neighbourhood councils discussed above would provide a source of more local comment. But an alternative approach, consistent with the pragmatic spirit of our proposals for initiatives outside the statutory services, would be to seek to establish rights to participation in those parts of the system with which the public is already familiar through its role as client and/or where the service is organised locally. Obvious examples are hospitals, residential homes, schools and area social service teams. We suggest three kinds of right need to be introduced.

First, the public-at-large in the catchment area of the institution should have the right to form a users' association. This would operate in many different ways, according to the interests of its members, but in all instances would be empowered to consult regularly with the management of the institution, to make recommendations to it and to inspect the operation of the institution.

Secondly, the clients of an institution or organisation at any one time should have the right to information on its management and to make representations concerning the operation of the service. These would be in addition to existing rights, which might well be further developed, for parents to be represented on the governing bodies of schools and for tenants to take part in local authority housing committees.

Thirdly, the logic of participation also applies to the employees of statutory organisations. At present few categories of staff, apart from powerful and prestigious groups such as the doctors in the health service, have rights to representation in the management of their organisations. There are several reasons why this position should be changed. As we have indicated in Chapter 3, bureaucratic forms of organisation consistently tend to under-use and alienate their lower-level employees by assigning them to highly subdivided and routinised tasks. Participative systems of management are one way of providing a more positive setting in which the employee can contribute to the organisation. Further, it would be unreasonable to expect staff to encourage user participation without recognising that they too had the potential to play fuller and more creative roles. We have also shown in earlier chapters that it is unrealistic to assume passive employee compliance with organisational demands; and, whether or not it is formally recognised, such compliance is the subject of a continuing process of negotiation. Participation does not remove the need for bargaining of this kind, but it does make it possible to carry it out openly, in a context where the problems facing both organisation and employees can be better appreciated.

For all these reasons the creation of rights for users should be matched with opportunities for staff of the social services to share in the management of their organisations. Again we resist the temptation to propose blueprints. Some of the schemes described in the previous chapter offer examples of how consultation and shared decision-making can be successfully developed in schools, hospitals and social services departments. There are numerous other examples of informal arrangements for involving staff in agencies throughout the social services. But we suspect they represent still no more than a minority of the total. While the particular form of participation should be worked out according to local circumstances, the right of staff to regular consultation should be recognised throughout all statutory services.

Cutting back the superstructures

If the main strategy for change is creating opportunities for people to act for themselves, as a counterpart it requires a programme for clearing the space in which local initiatives can grow, for felling and pruning the structures that overshadow them. Mrs Thatcher's government has made a ploy of attacking an ill-defined category of public bodies called quangos. In the process a number of relatively inexpensive, harmless and indeed mildly benevolent bodies like the Personal Social Services Council have been abolished. But much larger encumbrances of the governmental sector have hardly been touched. Near the head of any list of unnecessary governmental bodies must stand the Greater London Council. This has handed over most of its housing responsibilities to the London boroughs, and its responsibilities for the docklands have been taken away by central government. This has left it with only one field where political decisions are required – transport and roads. Yet, outside the housing field, it continues to employ some 20,000 staff, and it remains an organisation with large pretensions to governing London and to a strategic, regional role.

In practice, however, its pretensions are a facade that conceals an elaborate but usually ineffectual process of inter-authority negotiations. An illuminating study of the GLC's attempts at a metropolitan housing strategy (Young and Kramer, 1978) shows how the succeeding initiatives taken by the GLC from 1965 to 1977 disappeared in the sands of resistance from among the London boroughs and changes of tack by the ruling party at County Hall. Much of the energy of an authority intermediate between central government and the authorities with direct operational responsibility for most of the public services is bound to be absorbed in seeking co-operation and bargaining. This is conducive to the proliferation of bureaucracy, but not to solving problems and sorting out conflicts. The key point is that without an intermediate authority claiming a metropolitan role for itself, responsibility would rest clearly with central government, which has the real power in terms of legislation and resources to instigate the necessary action.

Although legitimated by four-yearly elections (the verdict of

which always goes against the government in power at
Westminster), the GLC is a remote and rather unreal entity for most
Londoners. Wherever there are real conflicts of interest it impedes
rather than facilitates the development of London strategies. Thus it
offers the appearance but not the reality of devolution from
Whitehall.

In Whitehall the Thatcher government has promised reductions
of staff. These may serve to reduce the superstructures, and by
limiting expectations of the functions of central government may at a
later stage offer more scope for the growth of decentralised services.
But the main changes that are needed are ones which would allow
the growth of community-based initiatives in territory now occupied
by the large local and health authorities.

Outline of a new structure

In order to give coherence to the policies advocated here a sketch or
summary of a possible alternative system is required. Its main
features can be subsumed under a number of points.

(1) Plural provision. A greater proportion of all forms of social
     service would be provided by voluntary organisations, the one
     major exception being social security. Thus instead of
     expanding the statutory services, there would grow up
     alongside them a variety of community-based initiatives.

(2) Decentralisation and community orientation of statutory
     services. The predominant mode of statutory provision would
     be the community-oriented one, implying flatter structures, a
     different interpretation of professionalism and reinforcement as
     opposed to replacement of informal sources of care.

(3) Contractual rather than hierarchical accountability. In return
     for funding and the contracting out of more services to
     voluntary organisations, government, both local and central,
     would exercise a stronger monitoring and inspection role than
     at present. Thus there would be more emphasis on maintaining
     accountability through contractual agreements as opposed to
     the exercise of authority within hierarchies.

(4) Participation in representation. The counterpart of greater
     monitoring and inspection would be the participation of
     consumers and providers in statutory decision-making. Thus

the representatives of users and providers would sit on local authority committees, and in the absence of, say, parents' organisations to represent parents on the education committees, nominations could be accepted from the generalist neighbourhood councils. This would mean a substantial dilution, or perhaps rather enrichment, of the pure doctrine of representative democracy: legitimacy would cease to reside exclusively with representatives selected by existing methods.

Making it happen

There are two objections to this strategy which deserve an answer. The first one is that the strategy depends on large numbers of people being willing to participate in one capacity or another in the running of the social services, whereas in fact the willingness to participate is limited. This objection applies to all more participatory forms of decision-making. Secondly, there is little evidence of a general demand for involvement, as opposed to a desire to influence specific decisions. Why therefore should any political party or government seek to change the situation?

The first question can be answered partly by saying that mass participation is not what is required. The existence of opportunities, or indeed rights, to participate and the use of such opportunities in a limited number of instances would alter the prevailing norms and the balance of power and expectations, and consequently the way in which larger parts of a system worked. This would permit the spread of schemes like those discussed in Chapter 9. But certainly the alternative strategy would require a higher level of sustained participation than at present. The reasons why people do or do not participate can be seen in terms of the costs and benefits to potential participants. How much does participation cost in terms of alternative uses of the time required and what is gained by way of better or different decisions and by the process of participation itself? For example, participation which calls for speech-making by people who have no experience of talking in public meetings, or involves long committee sessions at inconvenient times, and yet which seldom seems to have tangible results is likely to appear unattractive. But where the purpose of the exercise is clear and important, the methods involved are generally ones that people feel comfortable with and the chances of affecting the outcome are judged to be reasonable then good levels of involvement can be expected.

Experience of experiments in industry provides substantial evidence to support this position. Students of employee participation in management have found that when the organisation and management of work have been restructured to facilitate involvement in decisions over the immediate job, employees have generally responded positively to the opportunities (Argyris, 1957; McGregor, 1960; Likert, 1967; Paul and Robertson, 1970). Other studies have shown how employees themselves have sometimes taken the initiative to assume managerial functions (Blumberg, 1968). Some critics of the participation school have suggested that the significance of such involvement is limited since employees seldom show active interest in decision-making concerned with matters beyond their immediate workplace. But such attitudes could be seen as reflecting realism rather than indifference since in a capitalist or state-controlled enterprise employees can have no prospect of sharing in overall policy-making. This interpretation is supported by some research on workers' attitudes in Yugoslavia. There, all members of the enterprise are entitled by law to share in its management and interest in general issues of policy appears to be much higher (Abrahamsson, 1977, ch. 11).

There would seem to be no *a priori* reason why what is true of men and women as employees should not be true of them in their broader roles as citizens and users of the social services, if conditions to facilitate participation are created. Indeed, Chapter 9 has given several examples of active public involvement in the social services field where the gains from participation were made apparent and the means to hand were appropriate. Thus it is not unrealistic to expect wider involvement in decision-making provided it is organised in the right way and enables people to influence issues they know and care about. Beyond this, as we argue in the concluding chapter, it is not just a utopian dream, more a solution to the 'problem of leisure' to look forward to a time when, as the proportion of their lives spent on producing goods and services as employees in the formal parts of the economy declines, people will have more discretionary time and will use more of this to take part in public activities as opposed to private leisure pursuits.

The second question also exaggerates what is being argued for. What is envisaged is not the sudden radical transformation of the social services or the political system at large, but the strengthening of tendencies that already exist. During the 1970s a number of modest concessions were made to demands for more participation. In particular there is now wider involvement in planning and greater recognition that tenants should have a say in decisions about local authority housing and parents in the running of schools. Thus it is a gradualist, organic form of development that is being advocated, in character with the critique of past developments.

The fact that the changes are gradual ones does not, however, mean that the 'inevitability of gradualism' will work in their favour. This phrase coined by the Webbs related to their optimistic faith in the onward march of state collectivism. As we have seen, strong interests and commitments build up around large state bureaucracies which create a momentum for further growth. It is not clear that an equivalent momentum could be created in the opposite direction. While there is a strong body of opinion in favour of cuts in public expenditure, which is being actively promoted by the Thatcher government, a constituency that would lend weight to the sort of developments advocated here is more difficult to identify. Certainly it finds only a weak expression through existing political configurations. Thus it is difficult to envisage either of the main parties espousing these proposals as a major part of its programme for the social services, although they might be favoured by the Liberals.

On the other hand decentralisation and participation are not goals which any party would wish to oppose explicitly. And in a climate of scepticism about bureaucracy, governments could be expected to go on responding to demands for wider involvement. Indeed, because few such demands taken individually would pose a serious threat to central government, a piecemeal approach offers the prospect of some successes. In this situation there is scope for a movement for people's rights which would find expression through campaigns for specific rights. This must be the political strategy for the new radicalism advocated here.

CHAPTER 11

On Becoming
Keynes's Grandchildren

> The course of affairs will simply be that there will be ever
> larger and larger classes and groups of people from whom
> problems of economic necessity have been practically
> removed. (Keynes, 1931, p. 372)

The development of modern society can be seen as a one-way
process of increasing scale and specialisation, with more activities
steadily being absorbed into ever larger organisations. In Britain, the
first industrial society, this process seems to have gone farther than
elsewhere. The concentration of industry is greater and government
is particularly extensive and centralised, if not nowadays strong and
effective.

But there are signs that this trend is not ineluctable or irreversible.
Earlier in the book we introduced the concept of four sectors or
sources of social care: the statutory, the commercial, the voluntary
and the informal. Much of our critique has been concerned with the
tendency to rely unduly upon and to overdevelop the statutory
services at the expense of the voluntary and informal sectors.
Equivalent analyses can be made in other fields besides the social
services. Taken together the results of such analyses suggest that
there are undercurrents in advanced industrial societies which point
towards different patterns of development in the future.

In terms of general ideas the writings of Illich and Schumacher
have attracted widespread interest. There is also a growing body of
more sustained analysis which is undermining some of the
governing assumptions of recent decades. A significant part of it is
concerned with what is and what is not included in the gross

national product (GNP), the conventional summary measure of the country's economic activity.

Before continuing with our main argument it is necessary to say something about this. A number of terms are being used to distinguish the numerous activities not included in GNP. The black economy denotes activities which do involve cash transactions, but which are hidden from the authorities because they involve tax avoidance or other illegal activities. Theft and pilfering, prostitution and all sorts of moonlighting and odd-jobbing, the earnings from which are not declared for tax purposes, come into this category. Another quite different set of activities that also find no place in GNP constitute what is known as the household economy: that is, goods and services produced and consumed within the household, and not usually embodied in cash transactions. These range from all sorts of social care, through the preparation of meals and home-grown food, to the innumerable but growing variety of do-it-yourself activities. To these can be added transactions between members of the same family, even if they are not living in the same household. Thirdly, there are numbers of services provided outside the household or family setting, but which also are not embodied in cash transactions. These might be described as the voluntary economy. As well as services given on a philanthropic basis it includes all forms of non-cash exchange, from reciprocal helping between neighbours to house-swapping for holidays, along with participation in all sorts of organised self-help and voluntary activities. Together these three economies can be described as the personal or informal economy.

From its nature the size of the personal economy is very much an unknown quantity. Estimates by government statisticians suggest the black economy may amount to approximately 5 per cent of GNP (Macafee, 1980). All such estimates are subject to problems of definition as well as of calculating the quantum of activities that are not recorded. In Chapter 6 we summarised available evidence about the large amount of social care that emanates from the voluntary and informal sectors. It has its counterpart in fields other than social care. Thus productive non-market activities have been estimated in the USA to amount to nearly half of GNP (Nordhaus and Tobin, 1972). Although these are not much more than guesses, they indicate that the personal economy makes a very large contribution to the well-being of the population, even in advanced industrial societies where for so long the object of economic policy has been to maximise the measured part of the economy, irrespective of what happened in the unmeasured part. This has meant the transfer of many activities from the personal economy to the formal economy. But it has not all been a one-way movement. The growth of DIY exemplifies a movement of activities into the personal economy, as costs in the formal economy become too high and time spent in it declines.

A complementary question is to ask not about movements in and out of the personal economy, but about movements in and out of the formal economy. Putting it this way one can at least deploy some firmer data. For a long time there has been little change in the proportion of men who are economically active (i.e. in employment or seeking employment), except for the growing proportion of young people remaining in full-time education and a tendency towards earlier retirement. However, the proportion of their time that they spend in employment has fallen, with longer holidays and a gradual shortening of the hours of work. This decline has, however, been more marked among the working class than among the middle class. More recently there has been a large involuntary growth in the numbers not in employment with the failure of the economy to provide as many jobs as people want.

Among women the picture is very different. During the last century the proportion who were in employment declined, but since the turn of the century there has been a steady rise, discussed in Chapter 6, attributable essentially to more and more married women getting jobs. Thus as the level of participation by males has fallen, that by women has risen. Both tendencies have been much influenced by mechanisation in the home. Domestic appliances have made housework much easier, and along with control over fertility, have freed women for participation in the labour force. Conversely, the availability of electric tools has greatly helped men to carry out tasks in the home that would previously have been done by someone who was paid for the job. Thus changing technology can decentralise as well as centralise economic activity, and does not necessarily augment the formal economy.

In Chapter 8 we argued that our critique of the social services should not be seen in isolation from other trends, and that a number of the understandings that formed the basis for the postwar regime in Britain were becoming invalid. In brief, the state and the economy seem less and less able to deliver the goods. The assumption that people will acquiesce passively in the management of their affairs, whether at work or in the political arena, no longer holds good. This is despite the fact that ours can no longer be described as a full-employment economy and the projections which suggest substantially higher levels of unemployment in the future.

One set of responses to this situation is to reassert the importance of economic growth, and whether by state intervention or by freeing private enterprise, to seek to return to the rates of economic growth prevalent in the 1950s and the 1960s. This involves a reassertion of the role of the citizen on the one hand as a passive consumer of goods and services and on the other as an alienated employee in a large organisation. But there is another way of looking at the situation which sees our present discontents as creating positive opportunities for a change of direction.

What would this change of direction consist of? Answering such a question really requires another book. Here we seek simply to connect our arguments for alternative social policies with a set of wider issues concerning the shape that might be given to post-industrial society. In particular, one can discern three features in a possible scenario for the year 2000. First, formal employment would occupy a declining proportion of people's time. More scope would then be created for work which is not employment and for the extension of many aspects of the personal economy. Secondly, there would be a more critical approach to the development of advanced technologies; more attention would be given to their impact on the quality of life, on the environment and on the supply of finite material resources. The slogans here are 'appropriate technology' and a 'conserver' instead of a 'consumer' economy, which both imply smaller scale and greater self-sufficiency. Thirdly, instead of being a passive consumer of both political and economic goods, the citizen would have a more active role as a participator in political life and in his employing organisation, as well as through his own activities in the personal economy. This has radical implications for the management of industry and the rights of its owners, and for the nature of political democracy as well.

These priorities would sit happily with the strategy we have advocated for the social services. In contrast, a reassertion of the primacy of expanding the formal economy would limit the scope for community involvement in the social services; and although it would permit a pluralism achieved by contracting services out to voluntary organisations dependent on paid staff, the main weaknesses of the developments that took place during the past two decades would be unaffected.

It will, however, be argued that growth is the only way in which jobs can be found for the unemployed and for women seeking to emancipate themselves from domestic routine, and that more generally growth is a prerequisite if resources are to be distributed more equally within this country and if help is to be given to the Third World. These at any rate are the conventional wisdoms of what used to be the progressive consensus.

These do constitute sound arguments against deliberately intensified recession, but they do not justify making growth the over-riding economic priority of government. With or without a growth policy women will continue to benefit from the expansion of employment in the service sector, while even in a high-growth economy technological change means there will be insufficient jobs for the unskilled. In similar vein it is neither desirable nor possible for all the countries of the Third World to follow ever more closely in the footsteps of the developed nations. If only on account of the depletion of physical resources they need to devise their own technologies and social structures. Our capacity to help in this process could well be enhanced by the development of more appropriate technologies in our own economy and more participative social and political institutions.

An alternative economic strategy for Britain would seek to share employment among all that want it. Thus the number of hours' employment each week, the number of weeks' employment each year and the number of years' employment over a life time could all be reduced with the help of government action. Official policies could also encourage more sharing of employment and of other roles between men and women. Such policies could hardly be less successful than the policies for increasing the rate of growth pursued by successive British governments in recent decades.

No less important are the related arguments about equality. The necessity of a strong state has long been a fundamental tenet of most social democratic and Marxist thinking. But in seeking a strong state this body of doctrine has missed the point that the state machine is itself a source of inequality and has placed a premium upon economic equality at the expense of political equality. The notion of a strong people has, so to speak, been sacrificed on the altar of the strong state; and this perhaps is one reason why little progress has been made in either direction. Thus a redistribution of power between the state and the citizen is required on a much broader front than the social services alone.

In bringing this book to a conclusion we have deliberately

extended our arguments beyond the field of social welfare. We have endeavoured to show, at a necessarily superficial level, how the prescriptions we have advocated for the social services could and should be seen as part of a more broadly conceived alternative strategy.

It is hardly too much to say that in recent decades most of the issues so strongly contested in British society have been the wrong issues, that most of the defences from which the battles were fought have been death traps and that if there have been any victories they were Pyrrhic victories. It is not to be wondered, therefore, that ours is a time of uncertainty and demoralisation. Yet for us at any rate it is not without hope. Fifty years ago during the Great Depression, writing about 'Economic possibilities for our grandchildren', Maynard Keynes foresaw a not too distant future when people would be released by economic growth from scarcity and from the grind of always having to produce more and would instead be able to enjoy the good life. As Keynes's grandchildren we should grasp the chance to engage in fashioning a radical agenda appropriate to our times.

Bibliography

Abrahamsson, B, (1977), *Bureaucracy or Participation: The Logic of Organisation* (London: Sage).

Abrams, P. (1980), 'Social change, social networks and neighbourhood care', *Social Work Service*, 22 February.

Age Concern Training Department (1978), *Liverpool Good Neighbours Scheme* (London: Age Concern).

Allibone, A. (1979), 'How to cope with rural isolation', *General Practitioner*, 14 December.

Argyris, C. (1957), *Personality and Organisation* (New York: Harper).

Armstrong, M., and King, L. (1977), 'Schools within schools: the Countesthorpe "team" system', in J. Watts (ed.), *The Countesthorpe Experience* (London: Allen & Unwin).

Baker, J. W. (1978a), 'How a village helps the dying to cope at home', *Guardian*, 3 March.

Baker, J. W. (1978b), 'Care unlimited' unpublished.

Banwell, Sir Harold (1965), 'Report of an address to the Rural District Councils Association Conference, 1965', *Rural District Review*, August.

Bayley, M. (1973), *Mental Handicap and Community Care* (London: Routledge & Kegan Paul).

Bayley, M. (1978), *Community Oriented Systems of Care* (Berkhamsted: Volunteer Centre).

Beveridge, Lord (1948), *Voluntary Action* (London: Allen & Unwin).

Blau, P. M. (1963), *The Dynamics of Bureaucracy*, 2nd edn (Chicago: University of Chicago Press).

Blumberg, P. (1968), *Industrial Democracy: The Sociology of Participation* (London: Constable).

Brand, C. F. (1965), *The British Labour Party* (London: Oxford University Press).

Brothers, J., and Hatch, S. (1970), *Residence and Student Life* (London: Tavistock).

Brown, R. G. S. (1979), *Re-organising the National Health Service: A Case Study of Administrative Change* (Oxford: Blackwell).

Burns, T., and Stalker, G. M. (1966), *The Management of Innovation* (London: Tavistock).

Carter, J. (1981), *Day Services for Adults* (London: Allen & Unwin).

Cartwright, A., *et al.* (1973), *Life before Death* (London: Routledge & Kegan Paul).

Challis, D., and Davies, B. (1980), 'A new approach to community care for the elderly', *British Journal of Social Work*, vol. 10.

Chalmers, M. D. (1883), *Local Government* (London: Macmillan).

Chapman, L. (1978), *Your Disobedient Servant* (London: Chatto & Windus).

Clarke, F. (1974), 'Hospital at home', *Social Work Today*, vol. 5, no. 13.

Cochrane, A. L., *et al.* (1978), 'Health service "input" and mortality "output" in developed countries', *Journal of Epidemiology and Community Health*, vol. 32.

Collins, A. H., and Pancoast, D. L. (1976), *Natural Helping Networks: A Strategy for Prevention* (Washington, DC: National Association of Social Workers).

Cooney, E. W. (1974), 'High flats in local authority housing in England and Wales', in A. Sutcliffe (ed.), *Multi-storey Living: The British Working Class Experience* (London: Croom Helm).

Cooper, M. (1981), 'Normanton: interweaving social work and the community', in R. Hadley and M. McGrath (eds), *Going Local: Neighbourhood Social Services* (London: Bedford Square Press).

Crossman, R. H. S. (1975), *Diaries of a Cabinet Minister*, vol. 1 (London: Jonathan Cape and Hamish Hamilton).

Crossman, R. H. S. (1976), 'The role of the volunteer in the modern social service', in A. H. Halsey (ed.), *Traditions of Social Policy* (Oxford: Blackwell).

Crozier, M. (1964), *The Bureaucratic Phenomenon* (London: Tavistock).

Dalton, M. (1959), *Men Who Manage* (New York: Wiley).

Dearlove, J. (1979), *The Re-organisation of British Local Government: Old Orthodoxies and a Political Perspective* (Cambridge: Cambridge University Press).

DHSS (1973), *Review of the Home Help Service in England* (London: Social Work Service, DHSS).

Draper, P., and Smart, A. (1972), *The Future of Our Health Care* (London: Guy's Hospital Medical School).

Draper, P., *et al.* (1976), 'The organisation of health care: a critical view of the 1974 re-organisation of the national health service', in D. Tuckett (ed.), *An Introduction to Medical Sociology* (London: Tavistock).

Evans, E. J. (ed.) (1978), *Social Policy 1830–1914: Individualism, Collectivism and the Origins of the Welfare State* (London: Routledge & Kegan Paul).

Eversley, D. (forthcoming), 'Some new aspects of ageing in Britain', in T. K. Hareven (ed.), *Ageing and the Life Course* (New York: Guilford Dray).

Fabian Society (1980), *Evidence to the Labour Party Commission of Enquiry* (London: Fabian Society).

Finlayson, A., and McEwen, J. (1977), *Coronary Heart Disease and Patterns of Living* (London: Croom Helm).

Franks, H. (1979), 'Where life is still worth the living', *Guardian*, 9 January.

Friedmann, G. (1964), *Industrial Society* (New York: Free Press of Glencoe).

Gilbert, B. B. (1970), *British Social Policy 1914–1939* (London: Batsford).

Gladstone, F. J. (1979), *Voluntary Action in a Changing World* (London: Bedford Square Press).

Glass, S. T. (1966), *The Responsible Society: The Ideas of Guild Socialism* (London: Longman).

Goldberg, E. M., and Warburton, R. W. (1979), *Ends and Means in Social Work: The Development and Outcome of a Case Review System for Social Workers* (London: Allen & Unwin).

Goldthorpe, J. H., *et al.* (1968a), *The Affluent Worker: Industrial Attitudes and Behaviour* (Cambridge: Cambridge University Press).

Goldthorpe, J. H., *et al.* (1968b), *The Affluent Worker: Political Attitudes and Behaviour* (Cambridge: Cambridge University Press).

Goldthorpe, J. H., *et al.* (1969), *The Affluent Worker in the Class Structure* (Cambridge: Cambridge University Press).

Gouldner, A. W. (1954), *Patterns of Industrial Bureaucracy* (Glencoe, Ill.: The Free Press).

Green, G. (1972), 'National, city and ward components of local voting', *Policy and Politics*, vol. 1, no. 1, September.

Hadley, R. (1976), 'Beyond the limits of the welfare state: social policy and community resources', inaugural lecture, University of Lancaster.

Hadley, R. (1981), 'Social services departments and the community', in E. M. Goldberg and S. Hatch (eds), *A New Look at the Personal Social Services* (London: Policy Studies Institute).

Hadley, R., *et al.* (1975), *Across the Generations* (London: Allen & Unwin).

Hadley, R., and McGrath, M. (eds) (1980a), *Patch Based Social Services Teams: Bulletin No. 1* (Lancaster: University of Lancaster, Social Administration Department), January.

Hadley, R., and McGrath, M. (eds) (1980b), *Patch Based Social Services Teams: Bulletin No. 2* (Lancaster: Lancaster University, Social Administration Department), December.

Hadley, R., and Scott, M. (1980), *Time To Give? Retired People as Volunteers* (Berkhamsted: Volunteer Centre).

Hatch, S. (1978), *Voluntary Work: A Report of a Survey* (Berkhamsted: Volunteer Centre).

Hatch, S. (1980a), *Outside the State: Voluntary Organisations in Three English Towns* (London: Croom Helm).

Hatch, S. (ed.) (1980b), *Mutual Aid in Social and Health Care*, ARVAC Pamphlet No. 1 (London: Bedford Square Press).

Hatch, S. (1981), 'The voluntary sector – a larger role?', in E. M. Goldberg and S. Hatch (eds), *A New Look at the Personal Social Services* (London: Policy Studies Institute).

Hatch, S., and Humble, S. (eds) (1980), *Towards Neighbourhood Democracy*, ARVAC Pamphlet No. 2 (London: ARVAC Publications).

Hatch, S., and Mocroft, I. (1979), 'The relative costs of services provided by voluntary and statutory organisations', *Public Administration*, Winter.

Hazel, N. (1978), 'The use of family placements in the treatment of delinquency', in N. Tutt (ed.), *Alternative Strategies for Coping with Crime* (Oxford: Blackwell).

Heseltine, M. (1979), 'Why we must curb the bureaucrats', *Sunday Times*, 16 December.

Hewitt, S. (1972), *The Family and the Handicapped Child* (London: Allen & Unwin).

Hirsch, F. (1977), *The Social Limits to Growth* (London: Routledge & Kegan Paul).

Holme, A., and Maizels, J. (1978), *Social Workers and Volunteers* (London: Allen & Unwin).

Hoyt, D. P. (1965), *The Relationship between College Grades and Adult Achievement: A Review of the Literature*, ACT Research Report No. 7 (Iowa City: American College Testing Program).

Jacobs, J. (1965), *The Death and Life of Great American Cities* (Harmondsworth: Penguin).

Jencks, C. (1972), *Inequality* (New York: Basic Books).

Jones, G. W. (1972), 'The eclipse of Fulton', *New Society*, 17 August.

Kean, S. (1972), 'Towards democratic ward management', unpublished, London School of Economics, Social Administration Department.

Kellner, P., and Crowther-Hunt, Lord (1980), *The Civil Servants: An Inquiry into Britain's Ruling Class* (London: Macdonald and Jane's).

Keynes, J. M. (1931), 'Economic possibilities for our grandchildren', in *Essays in Persuasion* (London: Macmillan).

Lee, M. (1978), *Private and National Health Services* (London: Policy Studies Institute).

Leete, R. (1978), 'One parent families, numbers and characteristics', *Population Trends*, vol. 13, Autumn.

Likert, R. (1967), *The Human Organisation* (New York: McGraw-Hill).

Lupton, T. (1963), *On the Shop Floor* (Oxford: Pergamon).

Macafee, K. (1980), 'A glimpse of the hidden economy in the national accounts', *Economic Trends*, February.

McGregor, D. (1960), *The Human Side of Enterprise* (New York: McGraw-Hill).

MacPherson, C. B. (1977), *The Life and Times of Liberal Democracy* (London: Oxford University Press).

Makins, V. (1977), 'Countesthorpe College – the first five years', in J. Watts (ed.), *The Countesthorpe Experience* (London: Allen & Unwin).

Masterson, M. (1980), 'Legislating communities and neighbourhoods into being' in S. Hatch and S. Humble (eds), *Towards Neighbourhood Democracy* ARVAC Pamphlet No. 2 (London: ARVAC Publications).

Mather, H. G., *et al.* (1976), 'Myocardial infarction: a comparison of home and hospital care for patients', *British Medical Journal*, 17 April.

Meacher, M. (1979), 'The men who block the corridors of power', *Guardian*, 14 June.

Meade, J. E. (1978), *The Structure and Reform of Direct Taxation: Report of a Committee Chaired by Professor J. E. Meade* (London: Allen & Unwin).

Mellett, J. (1980), 'Self-help, mental health and professionals', in S. Hatch (ed.), *Mutual Aid and Social and Health Care*, ARVAC Pamphlet No. 1 (London: Bedford Square Press).

Midwinter, E. G. (1972), 'Victorian social provision: central and local administration', in E. W. Martin (ed.), *Comparative Social Administration* (London: Allen & Unwin).

Mocroft, I., and Hatch, S. (forthcoming), *Voluntary Organisations and SSDs in Two Authorities*.

Moroney, R. M. (1976), *The Family and the State: Consideration for Social Policy* (London: Longman).

National Consumer Council (1979), *Soonest Mended* (London: National Consumer Council).

Nicholson, L. (forthcoming), *The Arithmetic of the Welfare State* (London: Heinemann).

Nordhaus, W., and Tobin, J. (1972), 'Is growth obsolete?', in *Economic Growth* (New York: National Bureau of Economic Research).

Opit, L. J. (1977), 'Domiciliary care for the elderly sick: economy or neglect?', *British Medical Journal*, vol. 1.

Paine, T. F. (1974), 'Patient's Association in a general practice', *Journal of the Royal College of General Practitioners*, vol. 24, no. 142, May.

Paine, T. F. (1978), 'Inaugural meeting of the National Association for Patient Participation in General Practice', *Journal of the Royal College of General Practitioners*, vol. 28, no. 191, June.

180 *Social Welfare and the Failure of the State*

Paine, T. F. (1979), 'The patients' role', *The General Practitioner*, 14 December.

Parkes, C. M. (1979), 'The use of community care in prevention', in M. Meacher (ed.), *New Methods of Mental Health Care* (Oxford: Pergamon).

Parris, H. (1969), *Constitutional Bureaucracy: The Development of British Central Administration since the Eighteenth Century* (London: Allen & Unwin).

Parsloe, P., and Stevenson, O. (1978), *Social Services Teams: The Practitioners' View* (London: HMSO).

Pateman, C. (1970), *Participation and Democratic Theory* (Cambridge: Cambridge University Press).

Paul, W. J., and Robertson, K. B. (1970), *Job Enrichment and Employee Motivation* (London: Gower Press).

Pennock, D. (1980), 'Telegraph Hill Neighbourhood Council', in S. Hatch and S. Humble (eds), *Towards Neighbourhood Democracy*, ARVAC Pamphlet No. 2 (London: ARVAC Publications).

Ratna, L. (n.d.), *The Practice of Psychiatric Crisis Intervention* (Napsbury: Napsbury Hospital, League of Friends).

Reddin, M. (1980), personal communication.

Rees, S. (1978), *Social Work Face to Face* (London: Edward Arnold).

Richardson, A. (1977), 'The politics of participation: a study of schemes for tenant participation in council housing management', PhD thesis, London School of Economics.

Rutter, M., and Madge, N. (1976), *Cycles of Disadvantage* (London: Heinemann).

Rutter, M., *et al.* (1979), *Fifteen Thousand Hours: Secondary Schools and their Effects on Children* (London: Open Books).

Sainsbury, S. (1974), *Measuring Disability* (London: Bell).

Sanford, J. R. A. (1975), 'Tolerance of debility in elderly dependants by supporters at home: its significance for hospital practice', *British Medical Journal*, vol. 3.

Seides, S. F., *et al.* (1978), 'Long term anatomic fate of coronary-artery bypass grafts and functional status of patients five years after operation', *New England Journal of Medicine*, vol. 298, no. 22, June.

Shanas, E., *et al.* (1968), *Old People in Three Industrial Societies* (London: Routledge & Kegan Paul).

Shaw, H. (1978), 'How Kent found new homes for adolescents in trouble', *Guardian*, 22 November.

Silverman, D. (1970), *The Theory of Organisations: A Sociological Framework* (London: Heinemann).

Stanyer, J. (1973), 'The Redcliffe-Maud Royal Commission on Local Government', in R. A. Chapman (ed.), *The Role of Commissions in Policy Making* (London: Allen & Unwin).

Stevenson, O. (1973), *Claimant or Client? A Social Worker's View of the Supplementary Benefits Commission* (London: Allen & Unwin).

Stocking, B., and Morrison, S. (1978), *The Image and the Reality: A Case Study of the Impacts of Medical Technology* (Oxford: Oxford University Press).

Strauss, A., *et al.* (1971), 'The hospital and its negotiated order', in F. G. Castles *et al.* (eds), *Decisions, Organisations and Society* (Harmondsworth: Penguin).

Thornhill, W. (ed.) (1971), *The Growth and Reform of English Local Government* (London: Weidenfeld & Nicolson).

Titmuss, R. M. (1958), *Essays on 'The Welfare State'* (London: Allen & Unwin).

Titmuss, R. M. (1970), *The Gift Relationship* (London: Allen & Unwin).

Townsend, P. (1964), *The Last Refuge* (London: Routledge & Kegan Paul).

Townsend, P. (1965), 'The effects of family structure on the likelihood of admission to an institution in old age: the application of a general theory', in E. Shanas and G. F. Streib (eds), *Social Structure and the Family: Generational Relations* (Englewood Cliffs, NJ: Prentice-Hall).

Ward, C. (1978), 'Self-help socialism', *New Society*, vol. 44, no. 811, 20 April.

Warren, D. I. (1978), 'Explorations in neighbourhood differentiation', *Sociological Quarterly*, Spring.

Warren, J. R. (1971), *College Grading Practices: An Overview*, Report No. 9, (Washington, DC: ERIC Clearing House on Higher Education).

Webb, S., and Webb, B. (1923), *The Decay of Capitalist Civilisation* (London: Allen & Unwin).

Webb, S., and Webb, B. (1963), *English Poor Law History. Part II The Last Hundred Years*, Vol. 1 (London: Cass).

Weber, M. (1947), *The Theory of Social and Economic Organisation* (Glencoe, Ill.: The Free Press).

Whitehouse, A. (1978), 'Kent's good neighbours', *Community Care*, 22 March.

Wilson, A. T. M. (1977), 'Patient participation in a primary care unit', *British Medical Journal*, 5 February.

Wilson, A. T. M. (1979), 'What patients' groups can achieve', *General Practitioner*, 14 December.

Wolfenden, Lord (1977), *The Future of Voluntary Organisations*, report of the Committee on the Future of Voluntary Organisations (London: Croom Helm).

Wyvern Partnership and the Social Survey Unit, Birmingham University (1979), *An Evaluation of the Group Unit Design for Old People's Homes* (London: DHSS).

Young, K., and Kramer, J. (1978), *Strategy and Conflict in Metropolitan Housing* (London: Heinemann).

Official Publications

Bains, M. A. (chairman) (1972), *The New Local Authorities: Management and Structure. Report of the Study Group on Local Authority Management Structures*.

Bullock, Sir Allan (chairman) (1975), *A Language for Life: Report of the Committee of Inquiry appointed by the Secretary of State for Education and Science*.

Committee of Inquiry into Allegations of Ill-treatment of Patients and Other Irregularities at the Ely Hospital, Cardiff (1969), *Report*.

Committee of Inquiry into the Care and Supervision Provided in Relation to Maria Colwell (1974), *Report*.

Committee of Inquiry into Whittingham Hospital (1972), *Report*.

Department of Education and Science, HM Inspectors of Schools (1978), *Primary Education in England: A Survey*.

Department of Health and Social Security (1972), *Management Arrangements for the Re-organised National Health Service*.

Department of the Environment (1977), *Housing Policy: A Consultative Document*, Cmnd 6851.

Family Expenditure Survey (1977).

Farleigh Hospital Committee of Inquiry (1971), *Report*, Cmnd 4557.

House of Commons Expenditure Committee (1974), Session 1973–74, 3rd Report, *Postgraduate Education, Vol. 1, Report*, HC 96–1.

House of Commons Select Committee on Violence in Marriage (1975), Session 1974–75, *Vol. 1, Report*.

Maud, Sir John (chairman) (1967), *Report of the Committee on the Management of Local Government*.

Merrison, Sir A. W. (chairman) (1979), *Report of the Royal Commission on the National Health Service*.

Redcliffe-Maud, The Rt Hon. (chairman) (1969), *Report of the Royal Commission on Local Government in England*, Cmnd 4040.

Seebohm, Sir Frederic (chairman) (1968), *Report of the Committee on Local Authority and Allied Personal Social Services*, Cmnd 3703.

Social Trends (1979).

Index